First Printing: 2018

ISBN 978-0692052648

The New
P.O. Box 213
Midland, GA 31820

www.4thenewnu@gmail.com

get up and go!
Walking with God through the Perfect Storm

To my Father.
Thank you for finding me to be useful.

In a large house there are articles not only of gold and silver, but also of wood and clay; some are for special purposes and some for common use. Those who cleanse themselves from the latter will be instruments for special purposes, made holy, useful to the Master and prepared to do any good work. 2 Timothy 20-21

Contents

Acknowledgements
Introduction
Prologue

Chapter 1

Approaching Severe _____ *1*

Chapter 2

Severe _____ *5*

Chapter 3

Significant Severe _____ *8*

Chapter 4

Managing Emotions _____ *12*

Chapter 5

God's got it! _____ *20*

Chapter 6

Brick by Brick _____ *25*

Chapter 7

Completion _____ *33*

Chapter 8

New Beginning _____ *58*

After the storm a Calm

Chapter 1

    *Approaching Severe*_____ 63

Chapter 2

    *Severe*_____ 70

Chapter 3

    *Significant Severe*_____ 74

Chapter 4

    Dancing in the Rain _____ 81

Chapter 5

    The Call _____ 88

Chapter 6

    Nevertheless _____ 96

Chapter 7

    *Completion*_____ 109

Chapter 8

    *New Beginning*_____ 117

Acknowledgements

I am grateful to God who has done more for my family and me than we will ever deserve. I am also thankful for the James 1:17 husband, children, and grandchildren that He has blessed me with.

Thank you to my husband who is indeed one with me. I am honored to be your wife, your friend. To our oldest daughter, thank you for helping keep our home together during the first storm that I have written about. To our second to the youngest son, who slept in the same room with his big brother every night for days when we first arrived home, thank you. You stood guard and made sure his every need was met, thank you. To my daughter-in-love who drove miles to be there for her brother and sit with me in the waiting room and ICU for hours.

To the physicians, nurses, and medical staff who cared for our children, thank you.

To my family, mother, father, sisters, brother, aunts, uncles, cousins, friends, co-workers, son's co-workers, the driver of the other vehicle, doctors, nurses, neighbors, church family, strangers, and anyone who prayed with us, stood with us and believed with us, thank you.

Many dropped everything to travel and stand by our side doing whatever needed to be done. Others, cooked a meal, sent a gift card, provided us with accommodations, sent cards, texts, called, sent monetary support, or simply thought of us, thank you for allowing God to use you to bless us.

To every man, woman, boy or girl going through their own storm, may you find the source of the perfect peace that transcends all understanding. We are grateful for any part of our journey that helps you with yours.

Introduction

One of my favorite quotes is "A woman is like a tea bag; you can't tell how strong she is until you put her in hot water." I believe that only a person who has endured and learned from the discomfort and sometimes pain of being in hot water, in this case, Eleanor Roosevelt, could only speak these words. Much of what I share in this book is from my discomfort. Many of my experiences come from painful storms, storms filled with so much pressure that I felt like I had been steeping in hot water. Others came from making wrong choices and my Father, who knew that I would make them, weaving those mistakes and failures into His perfect plan for my life. I spent a lot of time questioning the reason for the storms or beating myself up over past failures. Finally, I learned that, as a child of God, every storm has a purpose and no mistake that I've ever made is wasted.

To put it another way, I've learned that God is the author of our lives, the Holy Spirit is the Editor, Jesus is the Administrator, and we are merely the Contributors. As the Author, God created our story and wrote the ending well before we were born. The Holy Spirit and Editor is responsible for correcting, giving guidance, and ensuring that the designed sequence is followed. As contributors, we can add to the story; however, our contributions cannot change the author's manuscript. In fact, as the Administrator, Jesus intercedes and manages our contributions. He makes sure nothing gets published that isn't a part of the original story. Together they make sure God's purpose and our contributions, both good and bad, follow the original storyline.

As I look back over my life, I see many dog-eared pages. Those are passages that I like to reread. I also have chapters I never want to revisit. I used to wonder why the Author included those sections and how they fit into the greater story. Each time I began a new and difficult chapter in my life, I was tempted to mark up the pages and ask the Editor for a revision. Somehow during the first sections of my story, I formed the idea that if God loved me, He wouldn't allow storms to interrupt and often devastate my life's story and those of the people I love. When I would hear other stories about babies being violated and abused, natural disasters, terrorist bombings or someone's diagnosis of disease, at times, something inside me questioned God's motives, His love.

I had this misguided perception that if I did what I was supposed to do, I would live an abundant life and be blessed. You know the pressed down, shaken together and running over kind of blessings. If things were going wrong, it had to be because I wasn't doing something right or because my faith wasn't strong enough. I mean, didn't Jesus die so that we could all live our lives free of difficulties and enjoy good health, a wonderful family, safety, a great career, a lovely home, and a nice ride?

Then, after steeping in that hot water time and time again, I became stronger and little wiser. I began to read the difficult chapters a bit differently. As the pages in my story became clearer, I realized that the joy and peace that I desired wasn't in living a perfect life. Instead, the perfect peace that transcends all understanding, you remember - the Philippians 4:7 peace, was in having an intimate relationship with God. It was in seeking and staying close to Him no matter what situations or circumstances come our way. This means relating to Him and everyone else with the same love that Jesus did. I now see that Holiness and happiness do not consist of living a mistake-free or pain-free life. Instead, this life is about loving the Lord with all our heart, soul, mind and strength, and loving our neighbor as we do ourselves (author's paraphrase Mathew 22:37) in good times and bad. Jesus came to give us the gift of a relationship with God, not the gift of material possessions or a problem-free life. Our role in this story is to learn how to stay close to Him, no matter what variety of blessings or storms come our way or what emotions try to consume us.

As I look at my life's story, I now understand that it has already been published. And unlike all the other books I have read, I can't skip ahead through the pages of my life to see what happens next. In fact, I rarely have the urge to anymore because I now know the Author personally and with each storm, I grow to trust Him even more. Although I don't know what's going to happen in the next chapter, I've read the original manuscript, and I know how my story ends...I win. (Romans 8:28).

I am sharing chapters from two of the biggest storms of our family's storms with the hope that others too will come to know the Author, the Editor, and the Administrator of their story in a whole new way. My prayer is that those who read it will be better equipped for their own storms. If this book is not for you, I pray that you will pass it on to someone who can benefit from it.

Prologue

On June 13, 2013, a severe storm hit our family and threatened to break one of the ties that connect us by taking the life of our oldest son. On June 23, 2017, we went through the eye of yet another very long storm with our oldest daughter. As I type this, I am becoming emotional all over again.

I originally wrote this prologue when I was several chapters into writing this book. At that time, I wrote **"I am overwhelmed with gratitude once again, knowing that I could be mourning the loss of one of my children right now. I could have mourned the loss of a child back in 2013. I could have had the daunting task of packing up their belongings to donate them to charity, could have picked out a headstone and finalized their last wishes...but God."**

I wrote the last three chapters of our story pretty much while it was happening. I stepped away from writing briefly only when our journey took an unexpected turn, and I needed time to process everything and readjust. During this time, God pressed more out of me than I ever imagined was possible. I am still overwhelmed with emotion and gratitude. This time, because He took our relationship to another level and through the lessons from the storms, He has set me free from yet another burden that I was never intended to carry.

This is how our family walked with God through two of our perfect storms.

Chapter 1

Approaching Severe

Fear of the storm is often worse than the storm itself.
Author Unknown

July 4, 2017

It happened again. This time I was driving to Atlanta when right in the middle of the four lanes of highway I started to notice clothes sprinkled across the pavement. It was as if a couple of suitcases had been opened and the contents were thrown from the window of a moving vehicle. As I slowed down to a near stop, I noticed the skid marks. Light at first, then dark and very curvy, showing the frantic attempts that had been made to stop the vehicle.

I felt my body tense up at this point as I inched closer. Several vehicles were pulled over with other concerned drivers running to a place my eyes had not yet focused on. Some were on their phones calling for help. Others were solely focused on following the path that the skid marks had taken, well off the road. Then I saw it. A van that had surely overturned and somehow landed right side up before hitting a tree. From my angle, every window appeared to be broken, and every airbag deployed. There were so many people on the scene that I didn't stop. Experience has taught me that there are times when our good intentions can become an obstacle when we don't pause to think about our next steps and our role in someone else's story. Often, we can stand in the way or delay what they need by trying to help. At that moment, flooded with emotion, struggling to catch my breath, I chose not to give in to my feelings. Instead, as I wiped the tears that had already started to flow down my face, and I prayed. I prayed for this person and anyone else in the vehicle. I prayed for their family. I prayed like I pray each time I drive up on an accident, only now I see their journey differently. Now, I know firsthand how quickly the forecast can change transforming a seamless, sunny day into a storm.

According to Wikipedia, "severe weather refers to any dangerous meteorological phenomena with the potential to cause damage, serious social disruption, or loss of human life." Severe thunderstorms can be assessed into three categories, Approaching Severe, Severe and Significant Severe. Like many people, our family has experienced all these storm types. Often it felt like we experienced more than our fair share. Our severe storms have included divorce, blending a family, rebellious teens, changes in income and employment, the sudden death of loved ones, church hurt, the substance abuse of loved ones and much more. With all of this, we had never experienced anything like the storms that were approaching.

get up and go!

It was Thursday, Junes 13, 2013 and it was a beautiful day. I remember this because after my morning devotion and prayer the next thing I do is open the shades to let in the light. We had had quite a bit of unseasonable rain, which kept things cool in Southern Georgia and helped me appreciate the sunshine even more. For the last few years, God has been working with me on believing Him and walking in His presence. On this morning I felt like I had taken two steps away from Him, so I prayed that God would empty my heart and my mind of me and fill them with Him. I prayed that He would help me to focus on all that I had to be thankful for. I remember after praying the thought entered my mind, no doubt in response to my prayer, "today you will rejoice." That's how God speaks to me sometimes, through a soft, peaceful thought that I know is not my own. Other times it's through my conscience, or through other people. Sometimes it's through His word.

After opening the shades in the dining room with my work clothes in hand, I moved to the kitchen to start some coffee while the iron heated. That's when our oldest son, James, came rushing past me with his clothes in hand. He moved the ironing board out of the laundry room/bathroom, so he could shower. I shot him a sharp look that said, how many times have I told you to allow extra time in the morning so you won't have to rush and now you are pushing me out...of my laundry room. He tilted his head down and gave me a childlike look as if to say, I know, I'm sorry. We had had this conversation verbally so many times that words were no longer needed. I ironed my clothes, grabbed my coffee and fruit and headed to get dress. That could have been the last time I saw James alive. Instead, as God planned, it was the last time that I would see him before we were both forever changed.

After getting ready for work I said goodbye to four of our six children, the fifth son lived in Fort Stewart with my grandchildren and daughter-*in-love*. I refer to her this way because more than law connects us. As I headed to my truck, I started to run down the list of all the things I was thankful for. I try to remember to do this whenever I feel any distance between God, which can open the door to so many other things like, doubt, worry, self-pity, fear, and lack of confidence. I remember being thankful for our health, home, and our neighborhood. We moved here from a crowded, noisy subdivision in 2007. Here it was quiet and peaceful with occasional deer running through our yard. Now our family could safely ride their bikes, walk, jog, or whatever. As I drove down the street, I rounded the last curve on what was once a 3000-acre plantation. It has now been transformed into a diverse community that comes together to

get up and go!

form a beautiful neighborhood. Here in this small town just outside of Columbus, Georgia was a backdrop of clear blue skies behind homes, green trees and flowers that looked like a work of art created just for me. My husband and I often joke that it should be called utopia, especially compared to some of the places we each laid our heads during rough seasons in our childhoods.

As I made it around the final curve on our street headed to the main highway, the storm hit. When severe weather hits, forecasters, news reporters, and geologists do what they can to give advance notice or to warn the public of the approaching storm. I have found the same to be true in life. There are times when my family had received such a notice, like when my grandmother was diagnosed with cancer, and we were told that she was in the final stages. Then we had two weeks to help us prepare, to equip ourselves, get things in order, and most importantly come together for our loved one. Other times, like when my father committed suicide in 2011, the disaster was sudden, unexpected, it hit hard, and it knocked the wind out of me.

With my father's death, God still wrote a passage into my story to prepare me for the coming disaster. As part of this plan, my pastor had asked me to baptize a child for the first time as youth pastor of our church. The young lady is still very dear to my heart, and I will never forget the closeness that I felt to God. In preparation I spent time meditating with Him, praying and worshiping and it was one of the times in my life that I could hear His voice the clearest. God knew just where I needed to be so that I would be positioned to handle the impending disaster. The baptism was Sunday morning. I received the call from my uncle, who delivered the news, shortly after I went to sleep that night.

As I look back over past storms, I can now see how each served their purpose to prepare me for this one. A storm I never imagined, when the flesh of my flesh, and bone of my bone would be broken.

get up and go!

Chapter 2

Severe

Sometimes God calms the storm, sometimes He lets the storm rage, and He calms His child.
Author Unknown

The windy road of our street intersects with a busy highway. And there it was, around the last curve before reaching the highway; I could see that the area was filled with emergency personnel. One officer was directing traffic while others were busy at work. There were so many vehicles that I knew it had to be a severe accident and I started praying for those involved. As I followed the directing officer's instructions, I turned right onto the highway and saw a wrecked van in the median on my left. As I continued, I saw in the short distance a small car that was a crumpled mess. I immediately started to pray for that person's family, thinking I don't know how they could have made it out alive.

As I got closer to the car, I lost my breath as I realized that it was the same color and size as my son's. I drove down to the next left turn in the median, stopped and texted my son James while I pleaded with God, "please don't let that be James, please don't let that be my son." I texted "James call me right now." Then I called and left him a message saying, "James call me and let me know you're ok." I called my husband who was on his way home from work and told him about the accident. I told him that I needed him to get there because I couldn't go back and find out by myself. When we hung up, he called James and texted him trying to get a response. In one message he said, "James if you are ok I'm gonna to kill you." I sat in fear for what seemed like minutes, and I said, "God I have to know, give me the courage to go back, be with me, and if this must be, help me." With that, I drove back to the scene, pulled up on the grass at the end of my street and walked up to the officer. I asked him if he could tell me what kind of car that was. He said why do you ask? I said because I think that could be my son. He said, "What is your son's name?" I said "James Manuel," and he said... "it is your son."

I immediately thought my legs would buckle under me. Just as quickly, it was as if God caught me and reassured me that James would survive this. It wasn't a small still voice; it was strong, firm, and powerful. Still, I wrestled with so many emotions as I struggled to make sense of this. Immediately after that, the officer told me James had already been taken to the hospital and only had a few scratches. For some reason, I was not convinced or reassured much by the officer's words. Maybe it was because I have learned by experience to apply the Latin term Nullius in verba, which means take nobody's word for it. In other words, see or find out first hand. Maybe it wasn't about whether I should take his word for it; perhaps it was simply the mother in me.

In the next moments, my husband arrived on the scene, and I shared what I had learned. We quickly planned to take his car back to the house and ride to the hospital together. My husband went over to gather

get up and go!

our son's belongings from the mangled vehicle, and one officer told him that after they were able to get the passenger side door open and get James out, he walked to the ambulance. This walk didn't seem extraordinary until we learned the extent of his injuries.

As I followed my husband home, I called one of my sister-friends to initiate our prayer circle. If you don't have one I recommend that you quickly become a part of one. One prayer has the power to change anything and believers joining together in agreement in prayer is even more powerful. I called my boss at the time, who is also a dear friend. These two calls ignited a circle a prayer and support that helped us through the storm. These two initially shared the news with others from our family, friends, church, and work families as we received more information. Each time someone new was contacted they immediately moved to do whatever God had already.

When we arrived home, our oldest daughter was about to take our youngest son to summer camp. I told her about the accident and told her to drive the opposite direction when she left the house. I didn't want her to see the car until we knew for sure how James was. I shared what we had been told about James condition, but it didn't comfort her. She is; however, is a very strong young woman and she pressed on like I knew she would.

get up and go!

Chapter 3

Significant Severe

Life's roughest storms prove the strength of our anchor.
Author Unknown

When we arrived at the hospital James' injuries were still being assessed. Within minutes the first ER doctor came out and said that James was still being examined, but they did know that he had some broken ribs. He said that the trauma team had been called in. Shortly after, my first sister friend arrived to stand with us. We then received news of a broken clavicle and a severely broken hip, but we were not able to see James yet. The news continued to get worse with each update from doctors, and God sent more of His people to stand with us. Before long the waiting area was standing room only and others were standing in the hallway. Friends, my co-workers, our son's co-worker's, and our church family poured in to pray with us, to feed us, to encourage, and to make us laugh. Yes, even then moments of laughter were so welcome. I should mention that other than my husband who is from this part of Georgia and his side of the family, before our marriage my children and I had no family ties here. Our only family was my brother, who moved from Fort Benning to another duty station a couple of years after we arrived in 1998. I mention that to show what a gift God has given us in the relationships; He has woven into our lives over the years. There are so many gifts that He has waiting for us, and often we miss them because we want to take control of our lives instead of allowing God to take the lead. He will often use unlikely and unexpected sources and resources to bless His children...when we let Him.

As the news became more serious even though my heart was broken for my son and I wanted so badly to see him, to hug him, to lay hands on and pray for him. I felt a strength that I can only explain by God's word. Greater is He that is in me than He that is in the world (1 John 4:4). It wasn't my strength that kept it together; I was cleaving to my Father and hanging onto His every word. I was standing with those who came as they prayed and gave God word back to Him. During moments that I didn't have the words to utter He sent others to intercede for me, for us, for James.

Finally, the trauma doctor came out and shared that in addition to the broken ribs on each side, a broken clavicle; and a severely broken pelvis, James had a fractured mandible, a collapsed lung, and some internal bleeding possibly to his spleen or liver. They needed my consent to proceed with the surgery intended to stop the internal bleeding and assess the other internal damage. The good news was that my husband and I were finally able to see James. I was so relieved to see my child. He was unconscious, had a tiny scratch near his nose, neck brace around his neck, and some swelling. Other than those things there were no signs that he had so much going on inside. We prayed over him, signed the paperwork and went back to wait.

get up and go!

After the surgery, the doctor came out with the results of the procedure and the other test results. He told us that James's liver and spleen had tears in them that were repaired. They also discovered that his diaphragm was severely torn and his stomach and intestines were pushed into his chest, his urethra was severed, and worse of all his aorta was torn. Then the doctor said they were not equipped to handle the severity of his injuries and needed to send him to the trauma team at a hospital in Atlanta. The challenge was that he wasn't stable enough to go by medivac because of the diaphragm injury and time was of the essence because of the tear in his aorta. They would have to stabilize him by doing the diaphragm repair here, and then get him to Atlanta for surgery to repair his aorta. The doctor also said that time was of the essence because if the aorta ruptured there was nothing that could be done. My husband and I went back to share this news with everyone waiting, and I could barely form the words between the tears and emotion. I choked out every word. Shortly after I gave the update, some of our family and friends stepped out to call others to update them on the situation. I was convicted for the first time to be the one to lead our next prayer before James went back into surgery. I didn't know how I would pray after barely being able to speak just moments earlier, but I was clear that praying was just what I was being instructed to do. I asked those who remained in the room to join me in prayer. I remember taking a deep breath, and the words began to flow out of me like honey. I don't recall what I prayed, but I know that there was a strength, power, determination, and a base in my voice that could have only come from one source. I know that I gave God's word back to Him and reminded Him of His promises to me. I know that I believed Him with all my being. I know that I could not have uttered a word aside from Him.

Soon after, we were guided to a surgical waiting room many times the size of the room we had just left. Nevertheless, before long half of that room was filled with more support and more prayer warriors. Our pastor was having a procedure done in Atlanta, so he sent others in his place to pray with us. Family, friends, and co-workers continued to come and stand with us.

Waiting at a time like that is so rough and painful. You are in a place where it is abundantly clear that you have no control nor does man. I cannot imagine how anyone makes it through this type of situation without God and the assurance that you don't know what the future holds but you know the one who holds the future. One of my sister-friends with connections to the hospital made sure someone behind the scenes gave us

get up and go!

periodic updates, so we knew the surgery was going as planned and he was stable. It seemed like an eternity before we were called back with the good news the operation was successful and they were loading James in the medevac to be transported to Atlanta. Hours had passed, and it was now early afternoon. I somehow convinced my husband, who worked 3rd shift the night before to get some sleep and drive up later. Two of my sister-friends had left the hospital as soon as they heard that James would be sent to Atlanta. Without giving it is a second thought, they went to pack their bags, pack my bags and get the car ready to drive me to meet James. As we watched the medevac lift off, I was so anxious to get going, wanting so badly to be there when James arrived yet knowing it was impossible because of the 1 ½ hour drive. I mentioned earlier that my pastor was in Atlanta having a procedure done, I didn't realize until we were in route that the timing of it was part of God's plan. He, our first lady, and their daughter were able to be at the hospital Atlanta in my place when James arrived.

When we arrived, we prayed, and our pastor and I were led back to James' room in the ICU. The trauma doctor told us that James was stable for now and they would monitor his aorta. As I understand it, they had to keep his blood pressure low to allow him time to heal without excess strain on his heart.

get up and go!

Chapter 4

Managing Emotions

There are some things you can only learn in a storm.
Joel Olsteen

In the first days after the accident, technology was both helpful and burdensome. My husband and I were bombarded with calls and text messages from loved ones seeking updates on James, and this was before news of the accident had fully been shared. I tried to create a group text to keep everyone updated yet it was still taxing. Then a dear friend told me about Carepages.com a wonderful free site where you can share your loved one's progress during times like these. Once I visited the site, I remembered that another family we are close to used it for updates when their son, one of James' best friends was in a horrible auto accident right after high school. The impact changed their lives forever, and their son has never fully recovered, yet they remained faithful and focused on God and His plan.

I immediately set up a page, and the result was overwhelmingly positive. Our friends, family and loved ones were able to get regular updates while sending messages and pictures to James and our family. The tool allowed me to focus on God and him. As I began writing the updates, God poured so much more into them. Those reading would post messages, text, and call to tell us how much our storm was blessing them. They would say things like, "the way you are handling your storm is helping me with mine." Some would ask for prayer saying, "I know your prayers get answered," "I know God hears you," or "I know you trust Him." You will find those updates throughout the next few chapters of this book, so you can better experience our journey.

My dashboard summary read:

This part of our journey began Thursday, June 13, 2013, after our son James purposefully survived a terrible car accident that occurred while he was in route to work. In Columbus, they attempted to repair his diaphragm and stop internal bleeding to his spleen and liver. The diaphragm surgery had to be repeated later (in Atlanta) with a more extensive repair. He was then flown to a hospital trauma unit in Atlanta to treat his injuries, with a torn aorta and hip treatment being a priority. His other injuries include a broken clavicle, broken ribs on both sides (every rib on his left side is broken). Also, every bone in his left hip is broken, he has three mandible breaks, a collapsed lung, a severed urethra, a torn aorta, and ruptured diaphragm with his stomach and intestines pushed into his chest. I am very specific about this because through this journey I know we will see what is not seen. Those who watch will see God knit James back together according to His workmanship! I believe it will be even better than when He knit James together in my womb!

get up and go!

On June 15, 2013, the trauma team physician believed James to be doing well enough to come off the ventilator. It turned out not to be a sound decision, and the extra effort required for him to breath tore the severed diaphragm that was repaired. His stomach and intestines moved back into his chest, and he was rushed in for emergency surgery. The doctors warned us that the area was so delicate after a second repair that they could not promise that it could be repaired again if this did not remain intact. As a result, they placed James in an induced coma and put a trachea in to allow the ventilator to stay in place for a more extended period.

It was during these times a roller coaster of emotions flooded me. Most of the time I was firm in my stance like a mother bear guarding her cub. Even though this cub was in his mid-twenties, I am sure that the instinct never goes away. With each unexpected twister came our way I initially became anxious, clinging to the reassurance and promise that I received while at the scene of the accident. Then I would pray and feel my strength and focus return, yet there was a part of me that still felt guilty for allowing myself to feel that way. I questioned if I doubted the God that had brought us through so many things. It was here that He taught me to give myself a break. God wasn't standing over me with some chart keeping a record of my performance, I was. Instead of focusing in on and trying to fix my mistakes and beating myself up over my emotions, He was encouraging me to fix my eyes on Him.

When we fix our eyes our emotions, they become overwhelming, and that puts us at their mercy. As I look back over the pages of my journey, there have been plenty of times when emotions felt overwhelming. There have also been plenty of times that I DID give in to them. It never went worked out very well. Then, little by little I began to understand the truth and the key to this lesson. The fact is that God wove emotions into us when we were knit together in our mother's womb. Without them, life would be colorless and dull. God intended for us to have the capacity to experience loneliness, sadness, fear, anger, pain, grief, fatigue, peace, joy, hope and love.

When we experience negative emotions, the key is to acknowledge them, allow ourselves to feel them but not to surrender to them. Not surrendering may sound simple enough; however, consistently applying these principles takes some practice. I can honestly say that God has given me plenty of opportunities to practice. My most significant came packaged as a beautiful newborn baby boy named Josiah. We welcomed our sixth child, Josiah, to the family through adoption when he was just seven days old. This little guy was just like the rest of the Manuel-Cooks

get up and go!

crew; he was perfectly imperfect. He completed us. I could and may write an entire book only on blending a family, although we likely have enough material for a series. For now, I will try to summarize.

For those of you who have blended a family, you know that it is not for the faint of heart. I can think of several scriptures that God may have had in mind just for this type of family, even if they were sometimes a reflection of His sense of humor. And yes, He definitely has one. Scriptures like: have I not commanded you, do not be frightened, do not be dismayed, or weeping may endure for a night, but joy comes in the morning. And of course there's, even though I walk through the valley of the shadow of death, I will fear no evil. I don't want to frighten anyone who is contemplating this bold move or discourage a family who has already stuck the mixer into the bowl, yet, it is a process. At times a painful one. You are combining two cultures and talk about having opportunities to practice managing emotions. Your emotions, your children's feelings and those of former spouses and their families. At this point in my life, I cannot fathom entering this type of relationship without being led by God to do so.

When we very prayerfully entered our marriage, the three children I birthed were young teens. The two he fathered were 4 and 7. Building a relationship with the little people was initially easy, although there were some bumps as they got older. On the first day, I won them over with some Bruster's ice cream and a play date to get to know one another. For my husband, on the other hand, it was tough. My daughter, the oldest, quickly came on board and loved him from the start. Her brothers, not so much. They were very protective of me after the divorce and didn't want any man around me. Then came the older kid's relationship with the two youngest, who all three of the teens only saw as pesky little kids. Often, the little people tried to get under the older kid's skin, once they learned that they could.

We saw from the beginning that this was going to be a process. It was like trying to blend cornstarch and water. Equipped with God as our parenting partner, my husband and I prayerfully agreed an insisted on two things during this period. First, they would treat one another and their belongings with respect. Second, and most importantly; we would not do "step." We weren't a "stepfamily," we were a family. The word itself brings separation. The third part of the Merriam-Webster definition is "the space passed over in one step." Think about it, where in the Bible is Jesus referred to as Joseph's stepson? He's not. Joseph fully accepted Jesus as his son. In the beginning, our children didn't know how to explain that they

get up and go!

had other parents without using the word. They soon became comfortable not having to explain themselves at all. We encouraged them that they didn't have to explain our world to anyone outside of it unless it was to educate. Those intended to understand will, even if it takes time. With that, I became "Mommy Tyila" to our little ones, and over time, my husband became "Pop" to the teens. Their choices, not ours. Our focus was on building an authentic relationship with one another, and that can't be forced. They were still very possessive when it came to my husband and me saying things like, "my dad said it's time for bed" or "my mom wants you." Those were signs that there were still some remnants of separation. Then came Josiah.

When we welcomed Josiah into the family, the last bit of separation left the household. Although they had already begun to form relationships before his birth, he was the arch that made the bridge between two separate halves stronger. I was no longer "mommy Tyila," I was simply mom. And phrases like "my dad" were exchanged for "daddy, or pop."

Our Josiah came with his share of obstacles to overcome. He is a fighter, which is why my husband nicknamed him Champ. Josiah was exposed to various illegal substances throughout the pregnancy, and they had an impact on his neurological system that manifested through his speech, occupational skills, temperament, and attention. We have researched to stay abreast of the latest educational and therapeutic resources. Our research helps us continue to step into this incredible young man's world and help him become everything that he was created to be.

Although there has been substantial progress, at six years old this is still difficult for him as a result of the speech delays he is working through. He often struggles to express what's going on in his world. In searching for an alternative approach to help him, I learned about Self-regulation. Self-regulation is the ability to manage your emotions and behavior in a manner that lines up with the demands of the situation. It is an approach that teaches even a child how to resist emotional reactions, how to calm yourself down when you get upset, and to adjust to a change in expectations and to handle frustration without an outburst. This set of skills enables children and adults to direct their behavior, despite the unpredictability actions and feelings of those around them. The practice encompasses acknowledging your emotions, allowing yourself to feel them and learning what steps you can take to keep from surrendering to them.

get up and go!

Acknowledge your emotions. At times our natural inclination is to shut down negative emotions. When we do this, we also cut ourselves off from the positive ones. Because the pain and pleasure centers of our brain are not entirely separate, it is believed that we can't be open to experience one without the other. In fact, for our well-being, positive emotions and experiences should co-exist with the negative, but they should also overshadow them. Acknowledgement is the first step to choosing which brain center will take the lead in your life. It allows us to look at the emotion in the face and say, "Your presence in my life is real, and guess what, that's ok." With this skill, we learn to observe our emotion, identify it and assign a name to it. For Josiah, he has a chart with sections for *what* he feels, *how* he feels and *actions* that can be taken to manage the emotion. In the first part, there are labels like mad, happy, sad and scared. His first step when a feeling arises is to name what he feels. For adults, we may use words like disappointed, worried and afraid. The most important thing is that the feeling is identified and exposed. That's when it starts to lose its power over you. Then you are ready for the next step.

Feel your emotions. God does not expect for us to go through life numb to the feelings that we have acknowledged, but He does intend for us to know the difference between what we FEEL and what we KNOW. For example, when the physician came in and told me that my son had to be rushed in for another emergency surgery and they placed him in an induced coma, I felt FEAR. I acknowledged it, and I felt it! On Josiah's chart, this section has pictures of emojis. One is beet red with a scowl demonstrating anger. Another has a frown and tears showing sadness; one shows anxiety, another fear and some are positive like a smiley face for happiness. The chart gives him the opportunity to identify *how* he feels. As simple as it may sound, once you have called out the emotion by naming it, expressing *how* it makes you feel leads to determining what to do about it. During moments of emotional stress, we experience all kinds of bodily reactions like increased heart rate, changes in our breathing, perspiration, trembling and even shaking. These are responses to how we feel. To keep them from overpowering us, we move to the next step and our focus on the actions or choices we can take to direct the feeling instead of allowing it to manage us.

Not to surrendering to your emotions. Emotions are influenced by our thoughts and perceptions. The way we perceive an event or interpret a situation opens the door to feelings that correspond to it. In Josiah's world, we are working to teach him to think about the way he will handle emotions before they occur. To accomplish this, the last part of his chart is

get up and go!

an action section. There are pictures of actions he can take when he is feeling an emotion. For example, if the emotion he acknowledged was anger, and the feeling he assigned to it was the beet red, scowling face, the action he chooses might be to go for a walk. There are other choices on the board too like taking a deep breath, doing jumping jacks, or having quiet time. Each time Josiah practices these skills his perception changes a little more. He is beginning to think about his feelings differently. Instead of focusing on how he "feels" Josiah is beginning to focus on what he "knows." What he knows is that he has other options for responding that leave him feeling empowered.

The same basic principle is true for us. After the initial feelings of fear that I felt when I spoke with the physician, God quickly reminded me of my favorite scripture, Isaiah 41:10. Fear not for I am with you, do not be dismayed for I am your God. I will strengthen you; I will help you, I will uphold you with the right hand of my righteousness. And there it was, in direct opposition to HOW I FELT, stood boldly WHAT I KNEW! God did not give me a spirit of fear. The fact is that any spirit of fear, doubt, worry, anger and so on, does not come from God. Instead, He gives us a spirit of power and love and a sound mind. Like Josiah, I had a choice to make and a perception to change in my thought process. It all started with an action, a decision to focus on what I "know" instead of what I "feel."

Jesus was the perfect example of this. He too expressed and experienced sadness, anger, pain, grief, fatigue, peace, joy, hope, and love. What Jesus didn't do was surrender to them. No, He did not succumb to the way he was feeling. Why? He knew that while these emotions are genuine, they are also unreliable. Instead, He lived out the truth of God's words.

Emotions can be affected by everything happening both inside you and around you. When we succumb, we let our emotions control us which puts us in an unhealthy position. When we, instead apply these skills we are empowered!

Please don't think for one moment that I have perfected this approach to managing emotions in my own life. No, there are times that I still succumb to the negative, only now I typically don't stay in that space for long. Like Josiah, I continue to practice. And I don't believe for one minute that practice makes perfect. Instead, I believe that practicing in a meaningful, methodical way (perfect practice) results in improvement, not perfection.

Our goal isn't to live a life free from negative emotions; it's to be one with Christ regardless of the sentiments we experience. Loneliness,

get up and go!

sadness, fear, anger, pain, grief, fatigue and other feelings won't be eliminated until eternity. As a result, to truly be at peace with our emotions and to be in control over them we must identify where they fit in our lives and learn how to deal with them. Choosing to acknowledge them, feel them and resist the urge to surrender to them helps us to find healing, peace, and joy, even in the middle of our storms. This lesson is a significant part of the foundation that equipped me for other storms, including the second one that I will share with you in this book.

get up and go!

Chapter 5

God's got it!

Don't tell God how big your storm is. Tell your storm how big your God is.
Author Unknown

During the first days after surgery, James slipped in and out of consciousness several times when he wasn't in an induced coma. Each time he was very groggy and initially, was startled each time he awoke; after all, he was waking up in a strange place, surrounded by strangers. When he tried to move, I could tell that he was feeling pain and he worked to adjust to limitations on his body. Some resulted from his injuries and others from various braces and bandages. He woke up to the rhythm of his breathing being unnatural as a ventilator and oxygen assisted him. After quickly working to process each of these emotions he would scan the room, anxiously searching for a familiar face. We would make eye contact, and he would relax a bit as if he was thinking, whatever craziness is going on, it will be ok, mom's here. I would quickly go to his side and calmly begin to share where he was and what had transpired. Then he would soon slip back into unconsciousness before he could absorb any of what I said. At least he heard my voice. James doesn't recall any of this, so he can't share his thoughts, feelings, emotions or recall the details of the accident.

Scientifically, as I understand it, when a person has been through something traumatic, often they don't remember what happened. At the time of the event, the brain isn't working on making memories. Instead, its focus is on survival. During those moments, the mind strips down to its most basic fight-or-flight response. Depending on the kind of event, this can help the person think clearly enough to take action during the situation effectively. Adrenaline starts pumping, helping them to react quickly and giving them extra strength to escape their predicament, all the while, hitting the pause button on memory making. I am grateful that he cannot recall those painful first days. I believe that is a gift intended to protect him. Although he can't remember the details of these moments, as a mother, I am confident of the feelings and emotions that I describe. Why? I know my son. I was there for each childhood scraped knee, bumped head, bruise, and sprain. I was there when he had to have stitches, ace bandages, and crutches. I know how he processes his emotions, how he freaks out at the sight of his blood, and how hearing my voice and seeing my face helps to ease the anxiety. It reminds me of how our God is there for me, for all His children. It reminds me of the story of Jesus calming the storm from Mark 4:35-41.

get up and go!

That day when evening came, He said to His disciples, "Let us go over to the other side." Leaving the crowd behind, they took Him along, just as he was, in the boat. There were also other boats with Him. A furious squall came up, and the waves broke over the boat so that it was nearly swamped. Jesus was in the stern, sleeping on a cushion. The disciples woke Him and said to Him, "Teacher, don't you care if we drown?" He got up, rebuked the wind and said to the waves, "Quiet! Be still!" Then the wind died down, and it was completely calm.

In this story, it wasn't the **absence** of the circumstances that changed things; it was the **presence** of God. He placed me in my children's lives as an extension of His love and to help fulfill a specific purpose in their lives. One of the things my presence says in their lives is, I can't take away the pain, for whatever reason, you must go through this, but you WILL NOT go through it alone. You've got this, and I've got you. The strength you need is already inside of you.

Shortly after the ventilator was removed prematurely, James woke up. For the first time, he remained conscious for several minutes. During that time, I was able to share the details of where James was and what had happened. I would do this several more times in the coming days because he just did not remember. After I shared, James had an expression that said, "really, an accident?" Then he rolled his eyes and tried to shake his head from side to side. James could only use his expressions because his mandible was broken in three places and he couldn't speak.

Next, Mr. WebMD as we like to call him because he is always researching the web and diagnosing himself began to conduct his assessment of his injuries. He could move one of his arms, although it was painful because of the broken ribs. The other was even more painful because of the broken clavicle. James slowly used his arm and finger to point to the areas of his body that were wrapped or sore, and he looked at me to explain why. My kids know me, I don't sugar coat what's going on. When they were young, if they were about to get a shot, I would tell them. If it was going to sting, I would say so. And I would say something like, "the sting won't last long, and you're stronger than this." Among the things I had already been praying for, I had specifically been praying for his mind, and I had my prayer circle doing the same. I firmly believe Proverbs 23:7, for as a man thinks in his heart, so is he. I knew that what James thought about the situation, his injuries and his ability overcome them was everything. I knew I had to get in his head with the truth before any thoughts of pity, worry, or anything else entered in.

get up and go!

And with a point of his finger down to the lower half of his body, we began. From the soles of his feet to the top of his head, limb by limb, injury by injury, I described them in full detail, and I told him about each treatment plan. The only information that I left out was the prognosis. To this day I find doctors' prognoses' to be humorous and a challenge for us to overcome. You'll learn more about why later. In short, I learned early on to trust the outcome of the Great Physician over all other theories or opinions. I do enjoy it when my Father blows their mind with one of His plans that exceeds reason or possibility. I also enjoy encounters with Godly physicians, those who have seen miracles first hand. They are quick to say things like, this is what the statistics say, now let's see what God says. Once we reached the top of his head, he paused. I knew he was processing all that I had described. I paused too, for a moment. Then, knowing that he was becoming overwhelmed, I said, "you are stronger than this." I reminded him that his body heals quickly, that he had healthy lifestyle habits before the accident that would aid in his recovery. I told him that this would be a battle of his mind and I needed him to keep his focus in the right place and on the right things. I told him that I would be with him every step of the way and most importantly, I told him that, "God's got it"!

He processed for another minute or so, and attempted to nod his head, yes! Then James made one last gesture. He took his hand, spread his fingers, and with his palm in front of his face, he made a circular motion around his face, then he gave a thumbs up. I chuckled because I immediately knew what he was asking. James was asking if there had been any damage to his face. Like the rest of his body, other than some swelling and that small scratch on his nose, from the outside, there was no sign that so much was going on inside. It reminds me of something I have learned and tried to teach my children. Never be envious of others, their possessions, accomplishments, personality or anything else. Often those who appear to have it all together on the outside are the ones who have the most going on inside. A troubled marriage, sickness, and life challenges that are far greater than your own. Instead, embrace your own story and always remember that things look a whole lot different from the driveway than they do from the hallway. Looking at his thumbs up, I chuckled again and said, "Your face is all good." We'll pray about that vanity later. James doesn't remember any of this even though I would repeat these steps a couple of times a day for the next couple of days, yet I knew that I was planting seeds...in good soil.

get up and go!

By June 17th the doctors believed James to be strong enough to begin the series of surgeries that would be needed to rebuild our bionic man. Although there were risks with doing it to soon, there was also the risk that waiting too long could negatively impact recovery to those areas. One of the most significant repairs was to the hip that was crushed. Metal plates and screws would be used to rebuild it. The prognosis...according to one surgeon, my avid jogger, would likely never run again and may have difficulty walking. I grinned as I prayerfully turned it over to God asking Him to show Himself strong and believing with everything in me that he would fully recover. He may even run faster after this! Below are my Carepages updates from this day:

Surgery Update
Jun 17, 2013
James is still in surgery to have the metal plates put in his hip. The Urologist came in just before they took him down and they are going to repair his urethra after the hip procedure. He has had four blood transfusions since he's been here; the good news is they have a good supply of his blood type. Thank you all for your prayers and support!

GGI (God's Got It!)
Jun 17, 2013
Update: The vascular surgeon will come sometime today to reevaluate James' heart. His primary doc says he sees no change in it, so J may need to continue with the blood pressure meds (to keep it low) for a while. He did say that J is doing remarkably well for his injuries to be as severe and extensive as they are. He also said we are not on the road to recovery yet. They consider that to be the time when all procedures are complete and true healing can begin. According to him, they are working in stages.

get up and go!

Chapter 6

Brick by Brick

Rise above the storm, and you will find the sunshine.
Mario Fernandez

When I was a child, our family struggled to find stability. For much of my early childhood, my mom was a single parent, and she was a very young mother. Most often it was just my mom, little sister and me. My mom longed to be healed from the wounds of childhood abuse and her longing for my brother, who spent most of his young life with our grandparents. Our mother's quest for love, peace, and fulfillment sent us on a journey from town to town, sometimes state to state and from one relationship to another. It was nothing for us to move several times in a single year. Financially, emotionally, and spiritually, we struggled. By the time I was a teenager she had begun to find the healing that she had searched for and in time, we all started to heal.

Through it all, I always knew that our mother loved her children. The difficult experiences produced some good characteristics in me, things like perseverance, courage, tenacity, resilience, and initiative. As my mother learned from her choices and experiences, I learned from my mother. Our world could crumble around us and while it may not feel good, just point us in the direction of the bricks, and we would rebuild. We often went *through* the *valley of the shadow of death,* but we had no intention of staying there. No matter how hard it was to climb out of the rumble, we learned to try. Those first steps were never easy but saying "can't" in my house was like a cuss word. We learned that if one door didn't open to lead us to the Brickyard, we needed to try another. God always made a way for us.

It reminds me of the book of Nehemiah. This book is a blueprint for rebuilding. It's the story of a man burdened with an impossible task, yet he relied upon the power of God to accomplish it. When Nehemiah was confronted with the task of rebuilding the broken wall of Jerusalem, he was shaken and nearly became overwhelmed by the size of the job. Along the way, he encountered resistance, criticism, personality conflicts, and financial pressure. With all of this, Nehemiah trusted God and led His people to complete the rebuilding of the wall and restore Jerusalem.

As for James, while his childhood was different than my own, he clearly learned some of these same lessons. Over the years he witnessed me, and his nana pull out blueprints and build many sound structures using love and forgiveness as the mortar to hold it all together. In the days following the accident, James demonstrated some of the same characteristics he had seen in us. Once he woke up completely and was able to remember the details I had shared many times, his focus was always on the next brick needed to rebuild. It took several blocks in the

get up and go!

form of surgeries, procedures, and therapy to put him back together again. God worked out every detail, just as He promised.

Surgery is Complete
Jun 18, 2013, 12:01 pm
James is in surgery; this is expected to take about four hours. The plan is to put two plates in his jaws, wire them shut, and put in the trachea, after all, to help wean him from the ventilator sooner. The doctors also hope to begin gradually transitioning James from the induced coma later today.

Jun 18, 2013, 2:34 pm
J remained stable through the surgery. The chin area of his mandible was completely detached so they had to add a metal plate on the left side and two plates to repair the three breaks on the right. He also has a fracture near his ear which is why his jaw will be wired shut. The wires will be replaced with bands in 4 to 6 weeks. He now has a trachea, and the ventilator is now attached to it instead of going through his mouth. We hope he will begin waking up sometime through the night or tomorrow. **Faith does not make things easy; it makes them possible.**

Jun 18, 2013, 6:01 pm
They have taken James off the paralytic. The first good signs are that he is starting to take a few breaths on his own. We believe that he will not need the respirator much longer. Please continue to join me in prayer for his peace of mind as James wakes up to a mouth that is wired shut, and we explain all that has taken place these past few days. **For God has not given us a spirit of fear, but of power and of love and of a sound mind.** 2 Timothy 1:7

Run Tell That!
Jun 19, 2013
This is the day that the Lord has made, and we will rejoice and be glad! James has woken up several times since last night. He has been able to nod yes or no to questions and guide us to where his pain is. As a result, more X-rays have been ordered to rule out fractures in his hands which are still swollen and according to him are painful. He will also have another CT scan later today to make sure the diaphragm repair is still healing correctly. James is fully awake! He has been able to write out questions with some of the first being, where am I; what day is it; and what happened? Is the other driver ok? And the all-important...can I have some underwear? They are

get up and go!

working to control the pain, and they plan to begin feeding him through his feeding tube soon. His fever has reduced! Please add to your prayer list that the risk of pneumonia will not come near him as a result of being on the ventilator for so many days.

Thursday Morning Update
Posted Jun 20, 2013, 5:21 am
"I have told you these things, so that in me you may have peace. In this world, you will have trouble. But take heart! I have overcome the world." John 16:33
James rested well through the night after a painful day yesterday. He is entirely off of the paralytic, so the pain was more intense. The CT scan and X-rays look good. There are no fractures in his hands, and his stomach is in place. He is still running a fever. Our prayer focus and expectation for today is that the fever will break and not return, the pain will be managed and continue to subside and that anything else that should be revealed and treated will. Also, that his diaphragm will continue to heal and be strong enough to sustain when he begins to be weaned off of the respirator later this week. We will also be agreeing for the renewing of James' mind, that he remains present focused and that the dew of God's love will refresh and strengthen his heart and mind.

As I reflected this morning on all that has transpired in the last one week ago, God laid the scripture above on my heart. During tragedy so many ask, "where was God." Too often I believe people make the mistake of acting as if God is a genie in a bottle. They put Him on a shelf until they need something and then run on trying to control all the choices in their lives. Then when trouble comes, they say "where was God." The answer is "He is right where you left Him." God desires to have a relationship with us. He wants us to trust Him and allow Him to lead us through each day. Instead of trying to work things out before their time has come, He wants us to learn to walk in His presence where we will find, peace, joy, and the fullness of life. When we learn to do this, as trouble comes, we are unmovable because we know that no matter what it looks like or feels like God's hand is in it even when the outcome is not what we hoped for or expected. When we grasp His hand in childlike trust, the way before us will open step by step. We will know that the One who has overcome the world will help us overcome our situation, in His way and time.

Have a blessed day family and friends.

get up and go!

Praising God!
Jun 20, 2013, 6:20 pm

Today has been a good day! Once James woke up he calmly assessed his wounds, and then he asked (by writing) how much progress he had made. I told him that he had made great progress and he said: "let's keep it moving." Two of his tubes were removed today, and he was able to have food through his feeding tube. I praise God for guarding his mind and heart.

Today I have been overwhelmed with gratitude and how great and mighty God is! How He loves us so much that He ordains every detail of our lives. As I continue to reflect on last week's accident, I can just see God and the angels assigned to James and me ready to move. At the point of impact, they were dispatched with their orders (FEMA ain't got nothin on God!). Then God reached down and snatched James from the hands of death so that He could begin to prepare Him for the next stage of his purpose in life. He is no doubt testing and strengthening me for mine as well in this classroom of His. Although I sometimes remind Him that I don't like some of the exams, I am growing to appreciate the lessons more. Remarkably we learned from the officer at the scene that James even got out of the car himself and walked to the ambulance with his extensive injuries and shattered hip.

Next God kept my legs from buckling beneath me when I drove up on this horrible accident on my way to work. When I caught a glimpse of the car, I started praying for the family sure that the driver of that mangled mess did not survive that. As I got closer, I quickly realized that my child, my son was possibly the driver. God ordained it that my husband drove up to the scene on his way home from work within minutes of this revelation. He served as my first earthly support. I believe God allowed that brief lapse in time to remind me that He had never left my side and it was His arms that held me first.

At the hospital, God quickly dispatched His children to surround us and offer support and encouragement. So many, so fast that the ER waiting room was standing room only. Even when we moved to the much larger OR waiting room, they continued to come until two spaces within the room were nearly full. At that time my heart ached and rejoiced at the same time. We rejoiced because there was no brain or spinal trauma and the spirit that God allowed to minister to me was saying that everything else will heal. Throughout each of James seven surgeries, God has blessed me

get up and go!

with a glimpse of His angels encamped around James in the OR and His spirit guiding all hands and all decisions.

I believe that in the beginning was the word, and the word was with God, and the word was God. As God took care of J last Thursday the word He gave me to meditate on was rejoice always, pray continually, give thanks in all circumstances. Friday the word was - have I not commanded you, be strong and courageous. The command let me know that it was not an option not to be and therefore I was. Saturday and Sunday the word was - focus not on what is seen but what is unseen, Monday it was - God's Got it! Tuesday - God has not given us a spirit of fear but of power, of love and a sound mind. Wednesday - this is the day that the Lord has made, and I will rejoice and be glad. As I meditated on Him, He took care of us. This is a small glimpse of the grace and love He has shown us, some of which came through the people He used, it includes:

The James 1:17 husband that He has blessed me with who keeps this family grounded on His word;

The sister and brother friends, who have cried, comforted, laughed, and celebrated with us. The one who was there to intercede and pray with me when a spirit of doubt attacked. They each have helped me to keep my focus, did praise dances in the OR waiting room, took care of details so I could focus on James. Some of them are a little on the bossy side (smile), and I love them all;

The angel He sent with water and notes of scripture and those who He sent for food and snacks while we were still in Columbus;

The mother, my mother (who is ALWAYS there for me) and family He sent from Tennessee;

The mother-in-law who is battling cancer in Tennessee and could not be here, yet she has sent every family member within a 300-mile radius to stand with her grandbaby in her stead;

The brother and sister in Washington, sister in South Carolina, the family in Indiana, Tennessee, Texas, Michigan, and Georgia who have traveled, prayed, and encouraged;

The Tennessee great grandparents and prayer warriors who have been on their knees for their gran even as one approaches his 92nd birthday;

get up and go!

The daughter-in-love, my little Ruth, who stayed by my side as long as the military would allow, and who has stalked me about her brother ever since she returned;

The one He sent with the foresight to make sure we had the funds, on the first day of this journey, to take care of any incidentals that immediately came up;

The moments when one of my sister-friends and I waited for James' 7th surgery to be completed. It was dreary and rainy outside as we sat in the hospital cafeteria. I simply said I wish the weather were better, so we could go out and get some air. Within 15 minutes the rain had stopped, the clouds were blue, and the sun was shining. Just for us.

The angel who graciously makes it possible for us to have a place to shower and rest;

The nieces who have called, prayed and served as babysitters;

The beautiful daughters and son who are holding it down at home;

The newly saved grandchildren who have instructed me to make sure I tell uncle James they love him and are praying for him;

Our Church family and all their prayers. Our Pastor, First Lady, and their family. As God would have it, his procedure was on the date of J's accident. This made it possible him and his family to be at the hospital when James arrived at the hospital in Atlanta while I was in route and desired to get there faster. What peace to know they were already there for him;

The ones who have offered up everything from air mattresses and collecting our mail, to blood donations for J's transfusions;

The countless people who have called or emailed their prayers and encouragement and to those who texted (including the funny messages that help us lighten up, laughter is good medicine;

The work-family that He connected me with as a source of income, and the kind of friendships that encouragement, love, and support flow from. James and I have been blessed with incredible people to work with, and... Benefits!

get up and go!

And finally, we are thankful for the peace of knowing that everyone who enters our son's room is intended to be there and will be used for such a time as this, whether they realize it or not;

Best of all we have the knowledge, peace, and understanding that He Ain't Done Yet!

get up and go!

Chapter 7

Completion

Don't let people pull you into their storm. Pull them into your peace.
Kimberly Jones

I am very interested in biblical numbers and their meanings. I met my husband on May 5, 2004, and we married on May 5, 2005. The number 5 represents "grace," and we love the thought of our marriage being covered by triple grace (5-5-05). Likewise, the number 7, like this 7th chapter, represents completion. Once the most significant surgeries were behind us, real healing began. During this time friends and family would text or post words of encouragement and prayers for James, and I printed them all. I put them on poster boards and displayed them around his room, so he could see the warriors standing around him to help him keep his mind focused. Guess what, it worked!

With each day, the storms of other's and their stories or prayer requests were written into our own. A hospital encounter, blog post or simply a text message saying, "I know your prayers get answered, please pray for me" would be incorporated into the book of our life. Our journey to this finish line still had a few twists and turns as you will see from the following posts that tell the story much better than I could recount it:

Breaking Every Chain
Posted Jun 21, 2013, 6:30 pm
I have been reading your messages to J, and he wrote out the following for you: "Thank you all for your love and support! It means the world to me during this time."

Js fever broke! Just like God is breaking every chain that binds him. Every culture and blood test is coming back good! Thank you for agreeing in prayer on that target!

He did have a rough night last and this morning. The trachea and respirator are irritating his throat, and he was experiencing reflux. One of my prayer warriors and I prayed over the situation around 8:00 and James has not coughed anything up since. They have suspended feeding temporarily to make sure everything is in order. They have reduced the ventilator to allow James to practice taking some breaths on his own.

The plan for tomorrow is to take him completely off the ventilator and give him oxygen instead. Our prayer targets for today are continued healing for every area of his body, the elimination of reflux, reinstating feeding and a smooth transition off the ventilator.

get up and go!

For God will break the chains that bind His people and the whip that scourges them, just as He did when He destroyed the army of Midian with Gideon's little band. Isaiah 9:4

Hallelujah is the Highest Praise!
Posted Jun 22, 2013, 10:55 pm

They took James off the respirator with the expectation of weaning him off in stages. The plan was to have him off for four hours and on for four. But God had plans of His own. James has been breathing well on his own, all day! He is doing better than was expected. The respiratory therapist just said "wow." He also resumed feedings through the feeding tube, and that is going well! The reflux and spitting up has not occurred again since my prayer warriors agreed with us! The X-rays continue to show that his lungs are free from pneumonia and his stomach is in place. We are praising God for continuing to show who is in control! Today's prayer targets are that J's white blood cell count will return to normal, that any infection must leave his body, and that his energy level will be restored. Thank you for standing, declaring, and believing that it's already done!

Embracing the process
Posted Jun 23, 2013, 7:55 pm

James is resting well today. He is completely off the sedation medicine and is adjusting well. His white blood cell count has not yet started to reduce; however, it had not gotten any higher. His temp has returned so they will start him on antibiotics as a precaution against infection. He still has quite a bit a fluid draining from around his left lung. Our prayer targets for the coming week are to continue progressing with his healing so we can transition from ICU, to reduce his trachea one to two sizes so it can begin to close, full function of his lung so the second chest tube can be removed. Also, we pray for J's temperature to return to normal, eradication of any infection trying to set up in his body, and that his white blood cell count will return to normal. We stand on Jeremiah 17:14 Heal me, O Lord, and I shall be healed; save me, and I shall be saved, for you are my praise.

Today God has been dealing with me on embracing the process. Mark 1:23 tells us "Truly I tell you, if anyone says to this mountain, 'Go, throw yourself into the sea,' and does not doubt in their heart but believes that what they say will happen, it will be done for them. Based on this scripture we sometimes speak to our mountains (our situations), and when they don't immediately move, we often begin to doubt instead embracing the process.

get up and go!

At times our mountains will move quickly, other times God wants us to put on our Timberlands and start hiking.

You see when we climb a mountain we step out of our comfort zone and off the beaten path where we must be alert to our guide (God), or we will get lost. Climbing strengthens our faith muscles and even if we stumble along the way God reminds us that He looks for persistence, not perfection. He helps us to focus on the unseen instead of what is seen. The higher we climb, the more spectacular the view becomes. Before you know it, we have reached our promised land. And we will be stronger, wiser, better, and best of all, the mountain has still moved, from the front of us to the back, where it now belongs.

I Will Not Be Shaken
Posted Jun 24, 2013, 6:48 pm
Find rest, O my soul, in God alone; my hope comes from Him. He alone is my rock and my salvation; He is my fortress, I will not be shaken.
—Psalm 62:5–6

James had a very rough and sleepless night last night. Seeing him go through was so hard, but with God's help, I remained unshaken. I knew if I was shaken then J would be too, and we need his mind to be strong to help him heal.

Sometimes it can be challenging to focus on the many things we have to be thankful for instead of the few things that are not going as we hoped. When we shift our mind to problems instead of thankfulness we open our minds up to darkness and self-pity. But when we have an attitude of gratitude we are setting the atmosphere for God to do His best work.

- *Today we are thankful for:*
  The prayers and encouragement posted on this site, the visits, the texts and calls, and the gestures of support. Our families, friends, church family, and work families who have shown up and shown out with even more love and support.

- *James' trachea being reduced (only two more reductions to go), the fever that has broken, his stomach and intestines starting to function more, a good report from the urologist and orthopedic doctors, and his mind remaining peaceful and focused.*
- *The peace that transcends all understanding, healing, grace, and mercy.*

get up and go!

- *The power of God that continues to move.*

Our prayer targets for today are continued healing of James' body and soul, and that God will begin to prepare the place in this hospital that James will transition to next. That the room, staff, and care on the floor will be exceedingly abundantly above all that we could ask or hope for. We also ask that you join us in prayer for Mr. Jerry who is in the room next to James. The doctors say his prognosis is not good...but God. And please pray with us for a lovely young friend of our family. She went to be with our Father this afternoon after a lengthy battle with cancer. While we rejoice for her, we pray for peace and comfort for her family - especially her young daughter.

My God is Awesome!
Posted Jun 25, 2013, 9:40 am

My, what a difference a day can make. After a rough night Sunday and pressing through, James slept like a baby last night! His white blood cell count is down; the fever has not returned and best of all...guess whose talkin!!!!

Speech Therapy put a cap on James' trachea, and we have heard his voice for the first time in days!!! He is doing so well that they are talking about transitioning him to the floor tomorrow instead of the end of the week. In fact, he's doing so good that the trachea they said would have to be reduced two more times before being removed, may come completely out by the end of the week!

We are excited about the possibilities and the promises! We don't know what tomorrow holds but the love and trust the One who holds tomorrow! I am overwhelmed by God's goodness and just how awesome He is.

No matter what your storm is, if you are a believer keep turning the pages of your book, weeping may endure for a night...but somebody knows like I know that joy comes in the morning!!!!

If you are not a believer, if you don't have a "relationship" with God, please feel free to contact someone who you know who has a relationship with God or me. We will pray with you and help guide you through your next steps.

Prayer targets: that we will find the right formula of nourishment for James, one that does not make him sick and that every plot and scheme that the enemy is devising is canceled right now in the name of Jesus. I

get up and go!

plead His precious blood over our family, friends, and this journey from beginning to end! No weapons formed against us shall prosper! We are MORE than conquers through Christ Jesus!

To God be all the glory! My God is awesome!

So Much to Thank God For!
Posted Jun 26, 2013, 6:12 am

After an amazing morning yesterday, it was as if God said, if you think that's good...watch this! He was encouraging me to continue giving thanks to Him so that James and I could enjoy the gifts waiting for us. God reminded me not to worry about tomorrow, instead to search for Him in each moment. That's where we would continue to find the gifts, miracles, and blessings that He created just for us.

Then He began to place gift after gift in front of us. In addition to talking, physical therapy came in, and James sat up, then he took three steps using a walker. The broken ribs, broken clavicle, broken hip, and wounded diaphragm didn't stop him! Undoubtedly greater is He who in James than He who is the world! Then he took a good nap like he had just run a 5K. :-)

Next, my work family sent James the most amazing and heartfelt video message of "encouragement in three words." I couldn't upload the video here, but you can see their wonderful notes by clicking on his photos.

Also, since asking you to pray for Mr. Jerry, the patient next to J who doctors were not sure would survive, he woke up and has begun to talk to his family!

And finally, a truck full of my sister friends and my niece surprised us from Columbus to keep us encouraged and to bring a gift basket of fruit from another friend. Thank you just does not seem like enough for everyone who has poured out, yet we say thank you! Praise seems so little for a God who has done so much, yet we continue to praise with all our heart.

Today we expect to transition to the floor, days earlier than expected. They are also telling us that with the progress J is making and the support system we have in place he may not have to go to a rehab facility once we leave the hospital, we can do his rehab at home instead. We continue to see new grace, mercy, and miracles each day. Every day it seems that a different member of his care team is saying "wow" to his progress!

get up and go!

Our prayer targets are continued healing for James and relief for his pain. We ask that all of the details, expenses, and filings pertaining to the accident will be worked out down to the last detail for James' good. We pray that James will be able to return to SCAD in September to begin his senior year as planned (the nurses are asking him to design some new scrubs), and we pray a special prayer for the healing of Ms. Liz (one of the trauma nurses).

We praise God for all that He has done and continues to do.

So Good I Just Can't Tell It All!
Posted Jun 27, 2013, 8:16 am
Give thanks to the LORD, for He is good. His love endures forever. Psalms 136:1

Good morning! And more Good news! After 14 days we are out of ICU! Also, J's trachea was capped off yesterday, and he is doing well with it which means we are expecting it to come out today. He will then be able to begin transitioning to the food he can taste, shakes and such, soon. We are also hoping that his last chest tube will come out today. They have shut it off, and so far, his lung is still inflated. Finally, he is receiving his new formula through the feeding tube well. In other words, our prayer targets are being answered! Thank you for agreeing with us!

Yesterday when I went to turn in my ICU visitation slip the desk clerk said, "You're leaving ICU, but you will wish you were back. The nurses on the floor each have up to 8 patients where here they have one to two, and the care is different". I said, "Good thing my trust is in God, not man." I believed what I said yet the enemy had a toe in and I started to worry a little about the possibilities. Our nurse then told me that they didn't have a private room for us which meant that I would not be able to stay with James at night. With his mouth wired shut I started to become anxious. His speech is low and muffled and asking for help or expressing his needs was difficult. And if he choked, would someone get there quickly enough. Then God reminded me that we have not because we ask not...and, so I asked. I prayed for peace, I prayed for help to remain focused on the present moment, and for a private room, excellent staff, and favor. I reminded God of the prayer targets my intercessors had prayed preparing for this transition, and I prayed His word. The anxiety quickly left me, and I was at peace knowing that we would either have a private room or God would give me peace in knowing that it was time for J and me to stretch in another

get up and go!

area. Either way, He had it, in His way and time. When we got to the floor around 1:30 this morning we were headed to the non-private room. We were introduced to the charge nurse. Just before they pushed the bed into the new space, she stopped and said, "Mom you like to stay with him at night right"? I responded, "I do." She said, "There is a room down the hall that was just vacated and cleaned, let's move there so you can stay and the two of you can be more comfortable." This room is private, with his own bath and shower, and he has a view of the city, and tonight's staff has been very attentive. We also learned that his trauma doctors will continue to treat him until he is released. That's grace, that's favor. That's God!

So Good I Just Can't Tell It All!

Our prayer targets are that the removal of his trachea and chest tube will go forth with ease, his lung will remain strong and continue to heal, and that anything that binds, any strongholds, chains, yokes, or generational curses that continue to bind him or our family will be broken. I pray that we will walk with confidence and boldness in freedom and on purpose for He whom the Lord sets free is free indeed! And finally, for the peace and protection of all of our intercessors and prayer warriors. I pray that God's richest blessings will pour out on them and their families.

Trusting God
Posted Jun 28, 2013, 9:36 am

James is resting well this morning. His trachea was removed yesterday, yay! And he had his first taste of food, which he handled well. When he saw the tray of broth, juice, and tea, he said, "This is so exciting." James has another day or so with the chest tube, but it's coming. The ENT docs have set a date to cut the wires in his mouth in about three weeks and add bands for a couple of weeks to allow him to begin moving his jaw gradually. White blood cell counts continue to reduce but are not entirely normal. He is fatigued and has lost quite a bit of weight. Most of all James is doing a lot of reflecting on what all of this (the accident) means in his life.

Yesterday was a chaotic day for the nursing team on this wing. They were short staffed because of last-minute challenges. The immediate impact to us was that when an alarm went off on J's IV, we waited 15 minutes without a response from the desk. While waiting, I called the two of the care team contact numbers and got no response. I had to find a nurse to assist. This happened three more times in a 5-hour period, once after I initially spoke with the charge nurse to voice my concerns. While I understand that these types of days happen in every work setting, including

get up and go!

my own, my mind began to wonder, and worry set in. As I voiced to the charge nurse, "what if" James had a critical situation and I had stepped out briefly? I needed to know that someone would be there to help him should he gag again from the new food or anything else and needed to be suctioned because his mouth is wired shut.

On the brink of escalating to another level in writing, God revealed to me that this was a test on trusting Him. When I prayed over these situations before we came to the floor had I relinquished all control to God or when things began to fall out of order would I try to take the lead in this walk to figure it out?

Apparently, I had not fully let go and had taken some situations back which led to frustration, doubt, and anger. My "what if" question was the first sign that the door of doubt had opened. I realized at that moment that God was calling me to be still and know that He is God. He was calling me to trust that He would take care of James no matter what man did and to believe that He had the unlimited resources and power to do it. God was calling me to trust Him in all situations, no matter what it looked like and not to waste my energy with doubt, regret, or trying to figure things out on my own. He was calling me to step back into the present moment and seek His way regardless of the circumstances. This is the place where He guards and keeps His children in constant peace while working things out for their good.

Our prayer targets for today are for James to continue to learn to listen to God's voice as He continues to speak to him. Praying for targeted healing for whatever is causing the elevated white blood cell count, fatigue, and low energy. We also pray James to regain the lost weight, and for a renewed and present focused mind for our family and us. And finally, we pray for supernatural healing for Mee Mee, a 24-year-old who was also in an auto accident and had to have an emergency surgery for a stroke that followed. Palms 46:10 "Be still and know that I am God. I will be exalted among the nations; I will be exalted in the earth!"

get up and go!

Walking by Faith
Posted Jun 29, 2013, 8:53 am
For we walk by faith, not by sight.
2 Corinthians 5:7

James had another day of good progress yesterday. He sat up in the chair for a while and took a short walk down the hall assisted by his physical therapist and walker. The staples from his diaphragm surgery were removed, and James continued well with his liquid diet. His white blood cell count has gone up, and he was on oxygen because there is an area of his lung that has not re-inflated. The good news is that once it does re-inflate his chest tube can be removed and a couple of days after that we can go home! Because he has a reliable support system at home, he will not have to go to a rehab center after leaving here. The doctors' hope he will be released before the 4th of July. Praise God!

We will continue to walk by faith, not by sight. We are depending on God and leaning not on our own strength or understanding, but His, which is limitless. God has promised to meet all our needs according to His riches. We "believe in Him" and nothing can change that. Faith means that we not only "believe in Him," it means that we "believe Him." Our prayer targets are that we command every disease, germ, infection or virus that has or tries to inhibit his body to be destroyed. White blood cell count must return to normal. Also, every part of James body including atoms, molecules, cells, tissues, organs, and organ systems will heal without setbacks and will function to the perfection that God created them to perform. James is under the manufacturer's perfect warranty! Psalm 107:20

Breakthrough Praise
Posted Jun 30, 2013, 9:43 pm

James had a good morning; he moved to the chair and sat up for some time. We are grateful for the angels God sent today to bring us a word, intercede in prayer and soothe our souls with song.

We still believe God for healing in his lung and the removal of the chest tube in God's way and timing. This evening he is experiencing a great deal of pain with his ribs. The doctor is trying a different medication to ease it. Also, we just received news that James' white blood cell count has gone up.

Now is the time that we are coming together for breakthrough prayer and praise knowing that God inhabits the praise of His people. Jericho didn't

get up and go!

just come down because of the marching; the walls fell because the sound waves collided with a wall. Sounds of praise blow up circumstances, break down barriers, and put the enemy on notice that God is bigger than anything he can throw at us!

Our prayer targets include relief from the pain and complete healing in James body. Also, we intercede with the family of Mr. Anthony. He is a police officer who was in a serious auto accident while off duty. We believe that he will walk again and that he will be transformed by the renewing of his mind. For both James and Anthony, we stand on Jeremiah 30:17 - But I will restore you to health and heal your wounds.

During this time, even after we left the ICU, God would convict me to go to specific places in the hospital where I would always cross paths with the person He intended me to. Even when we were in a private room, I never liked eating in front of James. I knew with his mouth wired shut he desperately wanted to taste something other than Ensure and other liquids. On more than one occasion when I would step out to eat God would guide me to a specific waiting room, usually back in the ICU. On one occasion I met a woman whose daughter was just a year younger than James. She had just been in a car accident and entered a place in the journey that we had just left. We talked, we prayed, we believed.

Yes and Amen!
Posted Jul 1, 2013, 7:47 pm
The chest tube is out!!! The white blood cell count is going down!!! Occupational and Physical Therapy and Orthopedics have cleared us to do our rehab at home!!! ENT and Urology have also cleared us for discharge. Our last step is to monitor Js lung for a day or two without the chest tube to be cleared by his primary trauma doctor, and we're outta here!!!

2 Corinthians 1:20 tells us that the promises of God are "Yea" (yes) and "Amen." Has He shown us miracles? "Yes!" Has He healed? "Yes!" Has He given us peace that transcends all understanding? "Yes!" Has He supplied all of our needs? "Yes!" Is He good? "Yes!" The promises of God are "Yes," and the promises of God are "Amen." And He Ain't Done Yet!

God, we thank and praise you with every ounce of our being!!!!
Our prayer targets: Praise, praise, praise for all that God has done and continues to do! We are praying that James will consistently continue to

get up and go!

progress with no setbacks. We are also praying for the healing of a young man named Karl.

There's A Praise On The Inside!
Posted Jul 2, 2013, 2:54 pm

We are going HOME!!!!

After nearly three weeks we are transitioning to a new path in our journey. It is impossible for me to reflect over this time without overflowing with praise! I cannot; I will not contain it! My heart has ached as I watched what was seen and it has rejoiced as God revealed what was unseen.

God continues to show us that praise and thankfulness lead to miracles. Yielding to His control and focusing on Him by rejoicing, praying, and giving thanks helps us to center our entire being in Him. This is how He created us to live. This is where we can enjoy the abundant life God has planned just for us.

Praise the Lord! Praise the Lord, O my soul! I will praise the Lord as long as I live; I will sing praises to my God while I have my being. Psalms 146:1-2

Our prayer targets: That our transition home will be a smooth one and that James will consistently continue to progress with no setbacks. We are also praying for the healing of Jaque, a 14-year-old who just had cancer cells removed. We believe that through this experience God will bring Jaque into a closer relationship with Him and Jaque will walk with God, even in his youth.

Resting
Posted Jul 6, 2013, 8:54 pm

Hello everyone. James is all settled in at home and resting much better here. He is so glad to be home, and I haven't appreciated sleeping in my own bed so much since my husband, and I returned from our trip to Haiti.

The last of his stitches were removed yesterday. In the coming weeks, the remaining wires and tubes will be removed, and we will shift our focus to physical and occupational therapy. His lung is still being monitored closely yet has shown significant improvement.

Now that our transition home is complete we are spending time this weekend resting. James is resting his physical body, and I am resting in God's presence. I am learning to embrace this time like never before to

get up and go!

refocus and refresh my mind. It serves to protect from all of the noise in the world that so easily distracts, and it equips for the rest of the journey.

"Be still and know that I am God; I will be exalted among the nations, I will be exalted in the earth."
—Psalm 46:10

Our prayer targets are: That as James heals he will continue to be transformed by the renewing of his mind. We are also praying for Kari, Jimmy, and their family. Their father is terminally ill, and we pray for God's to keep them in His comfort and perfect peace. We also pray for Nya, we pray that God will protect her, direct her, and guide her thoughts, decisions, and actions and that He will continue to give us strength and wisdom as parents.

The Eye of the Storm
Posted Jul 13, 2013, 7:28 pm
Hello family and friends. This has been a good week for James. He has continued to make progress with his walking, taking several steps a couple of times a day with his walker. James is so glad to be able to take regular showers and rest at home. He had a fever that came and went for a few days, but God answered our prayers, and it broke Thursday. He is having some pain and challenges with the urethra injury, which is our current prayer focus.

One of the highlights of this week for J was to have some of mom's hot cream of wheat through a straw. Seeing his pleasure at this reminded me of how much we take for granted. Another was a beautiful song and message of encouragement sent by video to us from a dear family friend. We are grateful for the continued prayers, calls, and texts of encouragement and the meals and fellowship brought by our dear friends.

The transition home has polished and stretched nursing skills that I have not used to this extent for at least 20 years, everything from J's injections to wound care. I am so very grateful to be positioned to be the one to care for him as he heals. It gives me such peace and joy.

I have had many people ask me about the peace that has encompassed me. I compare it to being in the eye of the storm. Just like in life, a hurricane or severe tropical storm can knock you off your feet causing extensive

get up and go!

damage, floods, flying debris and destruction. But right in the center of this severe storm is the "eye of the storm." Even though chaos is taking place around the "eye," here in this place it is calm, peaceful, there is usually no precipitation, and often the skies are blue. This is where God will keep you during your storm if you keep your "eyes" on Him. It reminds me of Matthew 8:24-26 when a furious storm arose that threatened to overtake the boat while Jesus slept. It that situation and in ours, it is not the absence of the storm that changes our situation, it's the presence of God.

Our prayer targets are total healing for James' urethra, safe travels, and God's favor as we journey back to Atlanta this week for a few follow-up appointments. We also pray for God's continued move and anointing at our church. Let it rain!

We are Grateful!
Posted Jul 18, 2013, 7:00 am

This has been a tough week for James. An ER visit Sunday confirmed that he has a severe urinary tract infection complicated by his catheter. This was the root cause of the fever and chills from last week. Tuesday, we learned that he was misdiagnosed and the UTI was not bacterial, but staph, which meant the meds he was given were useless and more aggressive steps, and meds had to be taken. He has been in quite a bit of pain.

We are grateful that God continues to be in control! It is no mistake that someone took a second look at those labs results. We are grateful that full healing is and will continue to come and God will continue to show His favor.

We are grateful that:
The wires came out Monday and James was able to open his mouth wide enough to eat mashed potatoes, pudding, and other soft foods for the first time since before the accident. Now we can get these 28 pounds back on him. He looks forward to grandma's cooking, Nana's mac and cheese, and Gran's sweet potato cake. The metal frames will come out in a couple of weeks;

- James was able to chew a French fry yesterday, by his reaction you would have thought it was the finest steak;
- Js general surgery follow-up went very well yesterday, and they were able to remove his stomach tube;

get up and go!

- *Family and friends continue to be so supportive with everything from meals, to gift cards for meals (which have helped so much with the back and forth to the hospitals this week), to cards, texts, calls, love, and laughter. God even sent Terese to the hospital yesterday, and she was a wonderful gift;*
- *New doors continue to open, and old ones continue to close;*
- *God has helped me keep my focus and bridle my tongue this week;*
- *Peace and joy continue to rain down on this family;*
- *We continue to receive reports of the answered prayers from those who have been included in our prayer targets;*
- *The best is yet to come!*
- *Please agree with me on this prayer: Dear Lord we thank you for your goodness, grace, and mercy! We are grateful that all power and authority is in your hands. We ask that you forgive us for any unforgiveness and anything that we have said or done that was not aligned with you and your will for our lives. We ask and believe that James will receive complete healing from this infection that will blow the doctor's minds. We ask for complete healing of the urethra injury and a smooth surgery to remove the catheter in August. We also pray for the following whose paths we have crossed on this week or who have asked for prayer (Sherieka, Sue, TR, Megan, Alisha, Terese and her daughter, Robert and his family, Chris, Freddie, Mrs. Gudger, and Jaque). You know their needs, and we believe that you will meet each need for you are Jehovah Jireh, the Alpha and the Omega, the one who was, who is, and who is to come, the Almighty. We stand on Hebrews 11:1 and we thank you and praise you in advance! In Jesus' name, we pray, Amen.*

In the Meantime
Posted Jul 24, 2013, 9:40 am
Psalms 130:5 I wait for the LORD, my whole being waits, and in His word, I put my hope.

We have made some good strides over the last few days. We were able to establish James' home health visits and have his initial physical therapy assessment. The RN who conducted Js initial assessment was going down his list of injuries, and she said, "I cannot believe that you were able to survive all of this, SOMEBODY was looking out for you." I don't know about you, but I'm glad to know that SOMEBODY!

get up and go!

J is still pressing through this infection. He is often tired, overall achy and his energy is very low. He does have a good appetite, so we should have some of that weight back up in a few weeks. Our next follow-up is with the orthopedic team at the hospital on Friday. We hope he will be able to begin bearing weight on his hip then.

As with other journeys, with this one, many of our prayers have been answered immediately while others have not been answered. What does this mean? I like to call this place "in the meantime." This is the time between praying a prayer and receiving an answer to it. I have found that it can be a rough place if your mind is not focused. These things have helped me maintain focus:

- *Remembering that a delayed answer is not a "no." God answers prayer in His perfect way and timing, often to prepare us to handle what we've asked for.*

- *Often after praying, we say that we are "waiting on God" when the truth is that God is "waiting for us." Waiting for us to let go of the things or people that don't line up with His will for our lives so that we can make room for our blessing. Waiting for us to believe Him. Waiting for us to thank Him for what He's already done. Or waiting for us to relinquish control of our lives to Him.*

- *Learning that when we let God guide us, especially "in the meantime" we don't waste "our time." Wasting time worrying, doubting, striving to force something that was not intended to be. Wasting time trying to figure it out on our own, or simply wasting what precious time we have on the wrong things. This also helps you remember not to depend on your own strength but to remember that greater is He that is in us than anyone or anything in the world.*

- *Learning to embrace the problems, tests, and trials so that they may serve their purpose to help us or someone else grow. When we run from them or face them with self-pity or negativity, it only lengthens the process and makes the storm more intense than it was intended to be. We often miss the lesson the first time and end up repeating it.*

get up and go!

- Remembering that sometimes a "no" will come. As I look back over my life, each "no" has been followed by something better than I ever imagined...in God's way and time as long as my prayers are aligned with His will. He doesn't always answer my prayers the way I initially envision but in one way or another God always answers my prayers. Even the "no" answers are for our good.

- Finally, with God as our guide if we do not quit, we will win. Romans 8:28.

We praise God for who He is, what He has done, and what He will do next!

Our prayer targets are that as we wait on the Lord, our strength shall be renewed. James' mind and body shall be stronger and better than ever before. That the good works God started with this journey shall be fulfilled.

Joy Comes in the Morning
Posted Jul 31, 2013, 1:18 pm

Psalm 30:5 Weeping may endure for a night, but joy comes in the morning.
James woke up this morning doing very well. He is working with his physical therapist as I type. This comes after one of our toughest days yesterday. We traveled back to Atlanta for the procedure to remove the arch bars from his mouth. Typically, the bars are wired across the patient's teeth much like braces, and then the top and bottom pieces are wired shut. Because of the extent of James' injuries (the entire bone under his chin was broken off, and he had a substantial fracture near his left ear) his bars had to be screwed into his gums. The ENT doctor told him that the Novocain shots would be more painful than just removing the screws encouraged him to proceed without it. The front screws were relatively easy, but the side and back were excruciating for James and seemed to go on for so long. I finally had them to stop the procedure and give him the Novocain. James was trembling and fighting back the tears, fighting so hard to be strong as a man. As a mother, this was one of my hardest days too. When they talked to him about the procedure, he looked to me trusting my advice, and I said it would be ok. Then it wasn't, and I was overwhelmed with emotion and guilt that I had encouraged him to make the wrong decision. As the procedure went on, he looked to me again as if pleading for me to help. Even with the Novocain I sometimes felt helpless and out of control. My strong, independent son is at this moment 27 pounds lighter, wounded, looks so frail is looking to be to be strong where he is weak. It broke my heart to see him go through more when he has already endured so much.

get up and go!

We were both very emotional afterward, on the way home, and into the evening. It was like the floodgates opened. We have been pressing on so much that I don't think either of us knew how much the other was carrying. When the floodgates opened all the feelings that we were carrying from these past weeks came pouring in. I believe we both woke up feeling cleansed and had a sense of renewal. We are filled with joy once again today! James has an appetite and is ready to press on. We both had a fresh perspective and renewed focus ready to run on and finish this race. No time for pity parties, guilt, doubt, or worry. I know who is in control, I will continue to put my trust in Him no matter what the situation looks like and He will see us through just as He has thus far. We will fill up with grace and pour out gratitude.

We have so much to be thankful for. James woke up with no pain in his mouth and has been smiling all morning, something he wasn't able to do with the bars in. He is eating well and took some steps down the sidewalk with his walker and the physical therapist by his side. His infection is under control, and he has new meds to control bladder spasms. His orthopedic doc has cleared him to begin putting more weight on his hip for the next six weeks and to begin transitioning to crutches as his ribs and clavicle allow. His wounds are healing faster than expected. We are grateful for every prayer that you have prayed; God has heard them and is answering! We are grateful for our two angels who stood with us yesterday and brought more joy and laughter before our appointment. Most of all we are grateful that God has brought us a mighty long way and He is not done yet! He will finish what He started and use this journey for His glory.

Our prayer targets are that everyone who has interceded for us and with us will be blessed beyond measure. For safe travels as we journey several more times to Atlanta in August. We pray that the surgery in Urology on 8/26 to be the final surgery. We believe God for complete healing of James' urethra injury that he will have full and independent function to this and every area of his body.

Nevertheless Faith
Posted Aug 2, 2013, 12:38 pm
"Father if you are willing, remove this cup from me. Nevertheless, not my will, but yours be done." Luke 22:42
Today we are about to head back to the ER after the visit from James' home health nurse. He was in a great deal of pain yesterday, and the bladder

get up and go!

spasms have returned, even with the new medication. His nurse suspects another UTI of some kind. As I reflect on the prayers that we have prayed over this injury, I am reminded of Jesus praying the scripture above in the Garden of Gethsemane. Like Jesus, sometimes we find ourselves in the Garden as we continue our journey. The question is will we surrender the outcome we think we want, based on our limited view of the situation, to God's perfect plan. This type of surrender requires "nevertheless faith." This kind of faith requires us to walk by faith, not by sight, to give thanks in all circumstances (which unleashes the power of God), and to follow while He leads, even when we can't see where we're going.

When we have this kind of faith, God empowers us to live above our natural ability. It allows God to work through us and fulfill His plans in His strength and in His time. It makes it possible for us to see every promise fulfilled and to receive every gift that has been prepared, just for us.

Our prayer: Great and mighty God, we come before you, humbled to be in your presence. We thank you for the prayers that you have answered and the works that you have done and continue to do. We ask for forgiveness where we have fallen short. Father we stand on Your word that says, those who know Your name will trust in You, for You, Lord, have never forsaken those who seek You, Psalm 9:10. We seek You and ask that if You are willing, remove this cup from James. Nevertheless, not our will, but Yours be done. We stand with the nevertheless faith that in Your time and perfect plan all things will work together for his good and your glory. In Jesus' name, we pray, Amen!

The Climb
Posted Aug 3, 2013, 4:54 pm

James is home resting today after a long day in the ER. They gave him some antibiotics by IV and thankfully released him to finish the next round of antibiotics by prescription from home. Neither of us could fathom the thought of another hospital admission. Our soon to be three years old, Josiah, can sense that James is not feeling well. It's so cute to see him go over periodically and kiss J on the forehead and rub his hand down Js face.

I heard a song last night entitled The Climb. The words are powerful, but I wanted to specifically share the chorus:

There's always gonna be another mountain
I'm always gonna wanna make it move

get up and go!

Always gonna be an uphill battle
Sometimes I'm gonna have to lose
Ain't about how fast I get there
Ain't about what's waitin' on the other side
It's the climb

In life there is always another mountain to climb, another situation to face. In my lifetime our family and extended family have faced everything from death, murder, sickness, and disease, to suicide. We often find that our mind is our biggest obstacle. When it's consumed with self-pity, doubt and worry or fear it can cripple us and keep us from stepping forward. Don't get me wrong, those emotions will come, and we must acknowledge them. But we must also see them for what they are and realize that they were sent to stand in our way, this will help us to overcome them. If not, they can bog us down, and we were not created to be bound by those emotions. Sometimes we want to take a detour, sometimes we feel like quitting, especially after what looks like we have lost. But if we just keep climbing, we always win. We win every time because we are stronger and better than when we started up the hill.

Our prayer targets are that James and our family will continue to have a sound mind and be fully equipped to finish this climb. We also pray for Cierra, her unborn child, her family and Dr. Allen who is dealing with the tragic loss of another patient this week who was in an auto accident.

For God hath not given us the spirit of fear, but of power, and of love, and of a sound mind. 2 Timothy 1:7 Inspired and Encouraged
Posted Aug 11, 2013, 11:37 am
Since my last update, James has faced new challenges and received new favor. Most importantly God continues to show us that He is in control!

During our pre-op visit with Urology on the 7th, we learned that Js urethra injury is more severe, rare, and extensive than was initially explained to us. We have learned that if the procedure is not done right the first time, it could result in ongoing challenges. As a result, the surgery on the 26th will be the first of the two-part procedure instead of the final one. The second cannot take place for two more months. For James, the immediate impact in his mind was the continued possibility of more infections because he will have to continue wearing the catheter during this time.

get up and go!

I am so inspired by his strength and courage throughout this process. He has his moments, as most would, when he is frustrated and discouraged, wanting to move past this place sooner. Each time he presses on.

We have also been told that there are only a few doctors in the US that specialize in repairing this type of injury. We praise God that one of the best will be doing Js surgeries and he has a high success rate (I've done my research.) They will also move the catheter so that it comes out of the bladder through the lower abdomen. This will be more comfortable for J and reduce the risk of infections.

We have also been working with SCAD, and a new door opened this week. They are going to work with him so that he can begin his senior year late next month! Now we are praying and believing that he will be well enough to be released by the remaining medical specialists to do so.
Our prayers targets are: For continued peace and clarity of mind and for God to eliminate anxiety, doubt, worry, and stress. We also continue to pray for the upcoming surgeries, dental implant, and remaining procedures and follow-up.

Lord, you are Strong and Mighty!
Posted Aug 25, 2013, 9:05 am
It's been two weeks since my last update, and God has continued to do a mighty work in our lives. James' infection is healed!!! He is walking on one crutch, which I to fuss to keep him on until orthopedics clears him Friday. We stand believing that they will. This has allowed him to get out between doctor appointments and physical therapy. We visited his work family a little over a week ago, and it did him so much good. I think he is still cheesing from that. The biggest part of his dental implant work is also now complete. I praise God to be able to say that we are down to our final stages of this journey. They are rehab, continued healing, and the final surgeries on his urethra. We will be heading back to Atlanta for the first of those surgeries; it will take place early tomorrow morning.

This week I have been reflecting on just how great, and mighty God is. As you walk through the gift that you have been given in this day, look up, look out, look around you. If God can create YOU and the heavens, sun, trees, and ground that you walk on, isn't He mighty enough to move in your life and situations. NOTHING is too difficult for Him! He carefully chooses the difficulties that He allows to come into our lives, difficulties sent to build

get up and go!

character. He also equips us to handle each and only asks that we trust in His strength and unlimited resources to see us through.

Our prayer targets are: That tomorrow's surgery will go according to God's perfect plan. That He is already setting an atmosphere of healing in this specific area of Js body. That He will guide the hands of and instruct everyone assigned to touch J or be a part of tomorrow's plans. That no weapon formed against us shall prosper as we continue on this journey. We also pray for the beautiful young woman who approached us at Walmart last night and her adorable baby. I could see God's spirit working through her and pray that He will continue to do a mighty work in her life. I pray that she and her child will be all that He has created them to be.

Be Still
Posted Aug 26, 2013, 11:29 pm
"Be still and know that I am God; I will be exalted among the nations, I will be exalted in the earth." —Psalm 46:10
James' surgery is complete, and it was successful. The doctors have taken some additional precautionary measures to help prevent other infections until the final surgery in 2 to 3 months. J is in quite a bit a pain tonight, and the pain meds have made him very nauseous. We are praying and believing God for a speedy recovery.

We praise God for once again answering our prayers and showing himself strong! We will also be still and rest in His presence.

Our prayer targets are: That God will move in the life of Brittany, a 22-year-old who has been diagnosed with cancer in her spine and various organs. All power is in His hands, and we pray His will to be done. We also pray for the release from orthopedics on Friday and that God will finish this mighty work that He has started in James.

Posted Sep 18, 2013, 7:18 am
This one is from James:

What I've been through the past few months is nothing short of a miracle and a blessing. I am so grateful for everyone's support and love. I know all the prayers were heard and they played a huge role in my healing. The amount of support I experienced was AMAZING!

To all the friends and family who traveled and took the time to write and call I want to thank you. I really have wonderful people in my life that care so much, and I love you all. I want to thank my church family for coming together and helping us in our time of need. Thank you to my work family for showing so much love. A big thank you to my work family, you guys helped lift my spirits and showed my mom so much support. A special thank you to Terese Young she was there to get me through some tough moments and helped take my mind off what was going on. I have also to thank my mother who sacrificed and loved me through this the way only a mother can. Without her by my side every step of the way I could not have made it. Thank you, mom, you are an AMAZING woman! I know this was tough for you, but you stayed strong for me, and I am so blessed to have you on my side. I hope I do not forget anyone.

The amount of love I was shown is overwhelming, and I am so very thankful. People always talk about things like the power of prayer or how through God anything is possible, but to actually live it and experience that power is a whole different thing. This has been a huge lesson in having faith and in knowing my own strength. I feel as if anything is possible after making it through!

James LL Manuel

get up and go!

I Believed
Posted Sep 18, 2013, 7:09 am
I had fainted, unless I had believed to see the goodness of the LORD in the land of the living. Psalms 27:13

Believing Him brought me through! Hello everyone, yesterday I took James to back to school in Savannah and left him. I have been emotional all week remembering how good God has been and how far He has brought James and our family. Our family celebrated as James pushed through his pain and what seem to be limitations and made the decision to start back to school. I wanted to shout as my child WALKED up the stairs to the room he will share with roommates. I said he WALKED! He is talking, and eating and breathing, things that were once, not long ago such a struggle. And he is in his right mind (most days). GOD HAS BEEN GOOD!

With all of this, I have still been emotional about dropping James off and leaving him. He has come so far, and yet he still has quite a way to go in this healing process. His endurance and strength are still rebuilding, as is his weight. James is easily winded as his lungs, once collapsed work hard to become stronger. Each step still takes so much effort as his hip, ribs, and abdomen heal. The suprapubic bag is still attached to help his body function, and yet it was time to leave him.

God once used my hands for his daily care, mouth for his voice, my feet to help him walk. He used my eyes to reassure him and now it was time to leave him. As hard it was to leave yesterday, I did. I left knowing that I was releasing his hand into God's, the only one who could ever love James or any of my children more than me. The one who knows the intricate design of the original pattern, because He created it. The one who is knitting him back together again.

Our prayer targets are: That God will continue the mighty work He has begun In James'. That He will continue to show His favor, grace, and mercy in James life. That James will be surrounded with the help, he needs when he needs it, and every door that God intends to be opened will open. We pray for renewing of the mind, protection as James journeys to and from school and protection over the house where he lays his head. Any new roommates who enter in must be a part of God's plan and will.

Thank you, family and friends. I will continue to post until after the final surgery.

get up and go!

Praising God!
Posted Sep 22, 2013 8:13am
James is celebrating his 26th birthday today!

I will praise God until there is no breath left in this body!

get up and go!

Chapter 8

New Beginning

Don't confuse your path with your destination. Just because it's stormy now doesn't mean you're not headed for sunshine.
Author Unknown

The number 8 signifies a new beginning. James' return to school proved to be a difficult one. His body was still healing and walking or riding his bike to classes took a toll. After the Fall semester, he took a break to finish the healing process. I do believe going back to school was the right decision for him at the time. It kept his mind focused on something other than his health and fueled his desire to live a full life.

Much has taken place in his life since the accident, new chapters for him to share when he is ready. I truly believe that my children's story is theirs to share in their time. Anything I write about our combined journeys is always with their blessing.

Now, five years after the accident, the skid marks have completely faded away from the accident site. When I drive by that spot, I praise God and pray that no amount of time will ever fade away the memory of our storm. I pray that my senses are never dulled to the joy I feel each time I see James go for a jog or accomplish a goal.

This will be one of the chapters in my life's story that I dog-ear and return to read often. I kind of see it as a jigsaw puzzle. From the beginning, God showed me the picture on the cover of the box, but the many tiny pieces inside hardly resembled this vision. From a natural eye, it was hard to imagine how they would form a picture. Many of the jagged, random pieces didn't look like much on their own, and it was sometimes hard to find where they fit in. Then God started piecing them together, and a beautiful work of art began to take shape. In His grand design, He made sure that not even one piece was missing, so the puzzle would not be incomplete.

Puzzles are a lot like life except most of the time we don't get to see the final picture of our story from the beginning. Instead, God gives us one piece at a time, just when we're ready for it. Once we've figured it out, learned how to add it to what we've already been given, He gives us another. We don't know how it will turn out, but God does. He created this amazing portrait on the canvas of our story before we were born because He so loves us. He knows just where each piece is intended to go and He's not the least bit surprised by the final work of art.

get up and go!

During the tough times, it's important to remember that they are just one piece of the puzzle and even in the toughest storms there are also pieces filled with joy, laughter, praise, grace, forgiveness and much more. If any of these pieces were missing, our puzzle wouldn't be complete. There will be some discomfort and some tough times as we work to make it take shape. We will make some mistakes along the way, no doubt placing a tiny piece in the wrong spot for a time, but no mistake that we make will ever be wasted. God will use it as a lesson to prepare us for the next piece, and the next. In time, our ability to assess each piece and carefully place it in its appointed spot will become better. We will become stronger and wiser, and our confidence and faith will grow. We will begin to see that God always goes ahead of us to prepare the way.

The most important lesson is to keep our focus on God, not the picture. He is the one who holds the pieces; He is the one that desires to be loved by us as we trustingly follow His lead in constructing the perfect image, a reflection of Him.

Live your life one piece, one day and one moment at a time. He has already worked it out for you and at the right moment, He will give you the piece with the answer you have been praying for. The one created just for you.

My final post:

Happy Birthday, Jesus!
Posted Dec 25, 2013, 8:12 am
Merry Christmas everyone! This is my final update. As this part of our journey winds down, it will forever be etched in my memory.

About a month ago James received the good news that he would not have to have the major surgery on his urethra after all. He was among a small percentage of people, who after having this type of injury, recovered without the need for the extensive repair. Yet another miracle! On the 19th he had a procedure to remove some scar tissue, and the results were very good. Today he will become catheter free for the first time in 6 months. A few follow-up activities and he will be knit back together, better than before.

Today we celebrate, we rejoice, we shout, we praise for all that we have witnessed these last six months, for the gift of James...for the gift of

get up and go!

witnessing first-hand the power of God and modern-day miracles! But most of all, for the gift of God!

The measure of our gifts was emphasized to us on Sunday when we arrived home from church. The intersection where James' accident took place was once again filled with emergency personnel because, yet another accident had taken place. Just feet from where he was t-boned, another driver and her passenger were t-boned as they left the church. This time the driver, a 78-year Sunday school teacher, died. Our heart goes out to her family as they mourn her loss.

We also think of the family of James' beautiful friend Vanisha as they spend their first Christmas without her. She supported James like a big sister after the accident, never realizing that she would soon be called home at such a young age.

I'm sure that if you were to ask Ms. Vanisha or the loving Sunday school teacher if they wanted to come back here to this earth, these daughters of the King would emphatically say "NO" with a huge smile on their face. Nonetheless, as we rejoice for them, they will be sorely missed.

The accident and those called home before we hope, they help to put things into the proper perspective. They help us remember that we only have one life, so we must live it. If we want to live it well, we must let God take the lead. And anyone who has made this earth their home really is "homeless." We don't know when or how our life will end, only that it certainly will. When it does, where will you go? Will you go home? Or are you "homeless"? (John 3:16 and Romans 9:10).

Thank you all who have prayed, stayed, laughed, cried, cooked, sang, and so much more! Our family is grateful that God sent you to us! For such a time as this!

John 10:10 I came that they may have life and have it abundantly.

Live your life!

Love the Manuel-Cooks Family

get up and go!

After the Storm is a Calm
Matthew Henry

Chapter 1

Approaching Severe

Even in the midst of life's storms, we have the capacity to stand in the center of God's peace.
Author Unknown

The Warrior. I once heard a story of a mighty warrior who had just married the woman that he loved. After the wedding ceremony, he and his bride headed out for their new home. The journey required them to cross a huge lake in an old wooden boat. As they were crossing a great storm arose suddenly. The warrior, a man who had been through many battles and endured many storms, was not shaken by the storm. On the other hand, his new bride lacked such experiences, and to her, the situation looked as if it were hopeless.

The boat was small, and the storm was strong and powerful. The winds blew and tossed the boat from side to side. It appeared as though at any moment the boat would be destroyed, and they would drown. Still, the man sat silently, calm and quiet, as if nothing was happening.

His bride was trembling, and she said, "Are you not afraid?. This may be our last moment of life! It doesn't seem that we will be able to reach the other shore. Only a miracle can save us; otherwise, death is certain. Are you not afraid?"

The man laughed and took his sword out of its sheath. His bride continued to tremble as a confused and uncertain look came across her face. The warrior then brought the naked sword close to his beloved's neck, so close that only a small space remained between the sharp edge of the sword and her flesh. As they stood there with this weapon that had been used in many battles almost touching her neck, he said," Are you afraid?" Immediately she exhaled, and her anxiety subsided while a loving smile came across her face. Then she said, "Why should I be afraid? If the sword is in your hands, why I would I ever be afraid? I know you love me."

He put the sword back, wrapped his arm around his bride, and looked her in her eyes. Then he said, "The same is true for me. I know God loves me, I know that He loves you, and this storm is in His hands."

The calm between our two storms came in 2014, and it ended in 2015. I don't want to mislead anyone into thinking that our family was living a trouble-free life during our "calm." To the contrary, we still experienced some rainy days. Remember, rain falls on the just and the unjust. In that season of our lives, God sent the kind of rain that patters against the leaves on the trees before falling gracefully to the ground. The kind that releases a sweet smell before it exits, making you appreciate the warm sunshine even more. It came in the forms of a change in employment for my husband, an adjustment in income, a boomerang child, grandchildren moving to another country, teenagers testing boundaries, a prodigal son, lessons to teach, lessons to learn...that kind of rain. Still, the reminders of storms from our past kept my heart grateful

get up and go!

and made me feel a lot like that warrior. At the center of everything we encountered, I knew God loved us and that all things were in His hands.

In 2015 our daughter and oldest child, Te'ashia, began to experience very serious changes with her health. She was diagnosed with Type I, insulin dependent diabetes at the age of 4 and by now the disease was taking a toll. During some of the 25 years leading us to this point, we were not successful in gaining good control of the disease. That coupled with the long-term effects of the illness resulted in vision problems, neuropathy, and high blood pressure in addition to diabetes and asthma. With all of this, the biggest blows to her health were yet to come.

Unlike the storm we walked through with our son, this one went on for years instead of months. Even though the level of intensity eased for periods of time, the storm clouds always seemed to be nearby, threatening to open without warning. In our later years, I often thought of and prayed for others with serious health conditions and for other caregivers who nurse elderly, chronically ill or disabled loved ones. The journey isn't easy for the loved one or the one providing care.

For those of us who are caregivers, many hours are often spent tending the needs of our loved one in addition to holding down a full-time job. I know firsthand that it's difficult to get enough sleep, and there is a consistent battle against things like stress, anxiety, mood swings, fatigue, and poor eating habits. Often, there is little time for the activities we enjoy, and if we're not careful, we can start to feel like caregiving is controlling our life. I experienced these very things along our path.

This part of our journey began back in 1990. I remember it well because my children's father (my former husband) was in the Navy. Shortly after our family relocated to Jacksonville, North Carolina he was deployed with his unit from Camp Lejeune to serve during the Gulf War. That left me there with our three children ages Te'ashia 4, James 3, and Terrance 18 months. I returned to our home state during the first couple of months after his deployment. That's where our village of love and support was. It included most of our family and our friends. Te'ashia began attending a head start program near my mother-and-father-in love's home where we were staying. Our first signal that something wasn't quite right came when she began having accidents at school. She had been potty trained since she was around 15 months old, so this was completely out of the norm for her. Te'ashia also complained of being thirsty all the time. Her grandmother and I still hate that we sometimes scolded her for the accidents, saying that she shouldn't wait so long to go to the bathroom. With her father gone, when this pattern continued we began to think that she may just be

get up and go!

experiencing anxiety or a UTI. She wasn't complaining of pain or discomfort, but I still thought it would be best if we returned home and had her examined at the Naval Hospital. My mother joined us on the trip back to help us get settled in. She watched the boys the day I took Te'ashia to the emergency room to rule out a urinary tract infection and to confirm that nothing else was going on.

On our way, I stopped and bought her a pack of Skittles. I watched as her face lit up at the thought of this sweet treat that she didn't have to share with her brothers. When we arrived, the doctor examined her, and the two of them were having a wonderful time laughing and joking as my very talkative little girl asked him a ton of questions. Do you have any Band-Aids? How long is this gonna take? Do a lot of little kids come to see you? What school do you go to? Thoroughly entertained by her, he answered each question while asking me a few of his own about her health history. The doctor told Te'ashia that he would need her to pee in a cup, so they could give her the right medicine. He told me that he too believed that it was simply a UTI. Before he went to check on other patients, Te'ashia had one final question for him. She said, "Am I gonna have to get a shot?" To which he looked into her little brown eyes and said, "No sweetie, I promise that you will not have to have a shot."

Little did we know that the climate we had become accustomed to in our world was about to change. We were coming from a place where the weather had been relatively steady for our young family. Now we were stepping into a valley that was foreign to us. It would be a setting where the temperature would frequently rise and fall, and the wind velocity would sometimes catch us off guard. In this climate, at a moment's notice, we could experience the effects of fog, hail, and frost. There would be a great deal of precipitation. In this valley, we would learn to look for the sunshine in an unfamiliar location, and we would treasure it.

When the doctor returned, his cheerful, fun-loving demeanor was replaced with a sad, solemn look. I initially thought that maybe something had gone wrong with another patient. He looked at me and said, "mom, we are going to have to run more tests, her urine showed that she has ketones in her urine." He went on to explain how ketones are made when the body breaks down fat for energy and how ketones are present when our bodies can't use blood sugar (glucose) the way it should. That's when this sugar spills over into the urine, something that is seen with Diabetes. As Te'ashia looked on, tried to make sense of all this and I said, "she had some Skittles on the way here so maybe that's why there is sugar in her urine. He assured me that this wasn't the case, but further tests would be needed to

get up and go!

confirm the real problem. Then he bent over to look into Te'ashia's beautiful eyes. The doctor choked on his words, and his eyes started to water as he said, "Sweetie, I was wrong; we are going to have to give you a shot." It's a little needle that we need to use to get some blood, so we can find out how to help you. Te'ashia started to cry, and so did I. The doctor took a deep breath and left before he followed suit.

The tests confirmed what that my baby girl did have Type I, Insulin Dependent Diabetes. Thankfully my mom had come with us. She was able to take the boys back to our hometown in Greeneville, Tennessee so that she and their other grandparents could care for them while we learned how to navigate in these unchartered waters. Communication to those deployed was very slow back then, and things were heating up with the conflict. Contact with your soldier was either through snail mail, the tedious process of going through his unit or contacting the Red Cross. We were instructed that last two options were for emergency situations only. It was also my understanding that these calls were brief. As much as this felt like an emergency, I reasoned that it would be best if I worked through this and sent letters, so I could share everything about what was going on and how she was.

Te'ashia was admitted to the hospital so they could stabilize her and determine the right regime of insulin. The task proved to be daunting because she was in what they called the Honeymoon Phase of the disease. This refers to the period after the initial diagnosis that the pancreas still produces some insulin. The pancreas produces insulin when it feels like it, which meant that it was easy to overtreat her by giving too much insulin and, at times, she would experience high blood sugars because she hadn't received enough insulin. I promise you that it was "no honeymoon." The medical staff prepared to educate me on managing the illness.

Even though I accepted Christ as my savior when I was a child, I was still a baby when it came to our relationship, and I was spiritually out of shape. Furthermore, I couldn't understand why God would allow my former husband, a trained Medic and a Phlebotomist to be deployed when he could have done all these things with his eyes closed. To say that this was emotionally and physically difficult for both Te'ashia and me is an understatement. I couldn't see it at the time, but God was working to strengthen my spiritual muscles. Right there, in the middle of this storm. God began by removing everything and everyone who I might be able to use as a crutch. As I look back, it was like He was saying, "It's just you kid and me. Welcome to the gym, I will be your personal trainer". Looking back, I now have a better understanding of His plan.

get up and go!

Think of the last time you went to the gym for a good workout. No, I mean really, with a personal trainer, not just dusting off your nice workout clothes and walking on the treadmill, like I sometimes tend to do. Personal Trainers, in the simplest terms, work to help others grow to the next level with their fitness. Most accomplish this by identifying where you are, helping you establish goals and by coaching as you work through a series of repetitions or workouts to reach those goals. Just when you start to become sore, your trainer will add more weight, reps or other challenges to increase the intensity of your workout. These activities are all intended to help us grow stronger and reach new fitness levels.

Spiritual fitness follows the same concept. I remember a well-known church and community leader talking about growth. He mentioned that many people get stuck in the same patterns or routines of life because they have become stagnant, complacent, too busy, or too scared to move beyond where they are. When this happens, if we are not careful we can allow someone or something within us to keep us from growing to another level. Too often what holds us hostage is nothing more than an illusion. It looks like an obstacle when it is not. It is fear meant to keep us from walking in our destiny. According to this church leader, his mother was an educator. As I recall the story, she desired for all her children to be able to count to 100 before they entered kindergarten. The leader, then 5 years old, struggled to accomplish this task. One day he went to his mother and excitedly shared that he could count to 20. To which his mother said, "that's good, but it's not good enough, you can count to 100." The illusion of an obstacle frustrated the young man until he realized that he didn't have to know how to count to 100 after all. Instead, he only needed to know how to count to 10 and start at "1" again on another level. That's all 11 is, it's "1"again, on a higher level. When we start on this new level it's not comfortable; it's not easy, you get nervous again, you get excited again. That's all part of living and growing.

Often God will use circumstances like a gym to help us break free from barriers and illusions. Sometimes our situations force us to go to "1" again. These hardships also push us closer to God. Workouts like these were very difficult for me back then because I was terrified of making a mistake. As a result, I resisted going to another level. I was a people-pleasing junky, and it took me a lot of years to break free from the opinions of others. It wasn't until I did break free that I truly learned to focus on God's opinion and pleasing Him. Breaking free helped me to embrace my mistakes, realizing that they didn't make me a failure; they made me a "learner."

get up and go!

Going back to "1"again also meant that just as any good trainer does, God didn't focus on the spiritual muscles that are already strong. To truly give me a good work out in His gym of life, He had to focus on my weaknesses. It didn't feel good and never does, but it made me stronger, and it helped to prepare me for the next level. Just like a physical workout, it was a process back then, yet over the years I have learned to embrace it. I now know I am producing new spiritual muscles each time He sends a new circumstance my way. The more it hurts, the stronger I am becoming. I remember hearing one athlete say, "I don't even begin to count the repetitions until it starts to hurt."

For my first set of reps, I needed to gain a better understanding of diabetes, my daughter's new diet, blood glucose testing, and how to give her an injection. The first few lessons were relatively straightforward, although overwhelming coming all at once. As for the injection, just the thought of it made me cringe. I didn't like getting shots, and I didn't like it when my babies did. Now I had to give them? The RN who was training me suggested that I practice on an orange to get the technique down. The problem with an orange was that there was no way to gauge if I was doing it correctly and I didn't want to hurt my child. Because of this, I practiced on my thigh instead. In the first days, even after explaining what we were doing and why it was important, it took me, two nurses and the doctor to hold Te'ashia still enough to give her the insulin shots safely. Now, I had to go home and give her these shots to her myself.

When we first arrived home, I explained everything over and over again until I was blue in the face. In the end, I still had to nearly sit on her to hold her still. I would make my sons go to their room, yet each time they heard their sister cry, they would open the door. Then they would stand in the hall cry and ask me why I was hurting her. Then I would cry.

I don't remember exactly how our breakthrough came, but it did. Soon, I would tell Te'ashia that it was time for her shot and she would come and sit down next to me and stick out her arm or expose another part of her body, so I could do what had to be done.

get up and go!

Chapter 2

Severe

She stood in the storm and when the wind did not blow her way, she adjusted her sails.
Elizabeth Edwards

As I mentioned, the first year was no honeymoon for us. Just when we thought our new routine was starting to form a new variable entered our lives, this one was called hypoglycemia. Hypoglycemia is the term used for low blood sugar. It was the most common complication of type I diabetes, and it entered our lives like an unwelcome and unexpected visitor.

I was lying in bed a few weeks after we returned home, and I heard a muffled moan coming from our daughter's room. When I went in, I found her nearly unconscious. Her eyes were rolled back in her head, and foamy saliva was coming from her mouth. I picked her up, and I remember saying out loud, "oh God, what is happening to my baby, please help me." There have been three times in my life that I thought my knees would buckle under the weight of a situation, this was the first. I carried her to the living room and called 911. I also called my neighbor to come and sit with my boys and as I tried to remember my training and what to do in this situation. Hearing about this and reading about it in a pamphlet was so very different than experiencing it. Still, with grace, I was able to gather my thoughts and follow the steps I was taught. She was not able to drink juice or to safely ingest the glucose cubes the hospital had supplied. Instead, I squeezed some of the gel I received into her jaw, but she couldn't swallow it. At that point, I knew we needed external help and prayed that the ambulance would arrive soon. They did arrive quickly, and within minutes of injecting Te'ashia with glucagon, which is a hormone that tells your body to release glucose (sugar) back into the bloodstream, she was up walking around. She had a headache, and a stomach ache which is something that would happen each time she received glucagon, but she was doing so much better. I, on the other hand, was ready for some of the water that Jesus converted at the wedding.

For months after that, our daughter slept in my room. When she returned to her room, it was with a baby monitor, so I could respond more quickly. Still, with each house that we lived in over the years, I'm certain that I wore a path into the floor with all the trips I made in the middle of the night to check on her. If I couldn't see or hear that she was breathing, I would lean over her to listen for her to take a breath. Once when she was a little older, she woke up and was startled by me standing there. She said, "Mom, please stop doing that," then we both laughed. On the other hand, during many of those nights, I was able to intervene when her skin was clammy or sweaty, and her breathing started to change, which indicated that her blood sugar was dropping too low. One time, I didn't wake up or go to check on her in the middle of the night. Thankfully, the barks of our

get up and go!

Cocker Spaniel Jackson, one of the kid's childhood pets, woke me up. I found him at the foot of her bed, unwilling to move until help came to assist her. It was a reminder to me that God always had her. The fear of not being there if she needed me during one of these times never fully went away, but from that day on it was no longer bigger than my God.

In the fall, Te'ashia started kindergarten, and I cried as my baby girl climbed on that bus. Later in the week, I received the first of 5 calls from the nurse telling me that Te'ashia was having a hypoglycemic reaction that they were not able to treat, and she was on her way to the hospital in an ambulance. Even though I was doing everything I knew to do, I felt horrible. It seemed like no matter what I did, monitoring, making sure she had the right foods and timely injections, her blood sugars still fluctuated from one end of the scale to the other. In the absence of the knowledge and technological advancements of today, things that would have changed our world, I was frustrated.

Even with all of this, at 4, her spirit and strength started to show more clearly. Seeing these qualities in her inspired us during this tough time for our family. In fact, once my child had a chance to process this whole thing, she took hold of it, it didn't hold her. Te'ashia didn't cry or complain anymore about receiving multiple injections each day and never fussed about her fingers being sore from the many finger pricks to check blood sugar levels. When it was time to draw blood during doctor visits, she would climb into a chair, often next to a young soldier who was also having blood drawn. The nurses would comment about how brave she was as she stretched out her little arm to be stuck. They would often use her as an example when the soldier sitting next to her began to flinch or grimace during the process. Te'ashia would smile and say; my daddy draws blood too.

Her doctor's visits were often entertaining as well. During one follow-up visit, a younger physician was standing in for Te'ashia's regular doctor. I watched, thoroughly entertained as my inquisitive child held a very interesting conversation with the young physician. She began by observing him quietly as if she was critiquing his methods. Then she said, "how old are you?" When he responded by telling her that he was almost 30, she carefully folded her arms across her chest and followed with, "well, how long have you been a doctor?" The doctor, who was also entertained at this point, grinned and said, "not very long." Then, to my surprise, Te'ashia went on to proudly tell this physician that her papa was also a doctor. Which, by the way, he wasn't! My children's grandfather, their papa, was named after his father. He went by the name J.V., which stood

get up and go!

for Jessie Verna and jokingly referred to himself as "Dr. J" to his grandchildren.

At that point, my expression turned from one of amusement to shock. Curiously, the doctor said, "oh really, what kind of doctor is he?" My eyes got big and as we both looked at her and waited for a response. I couldn't wait to hear this. Without missing a beat, she boldly and confidently said, "He's a Dr. J." I tried so hard to contain my laughter. But one thing was certain; I was not about to interfere the way she viewed her beloved papa. Besides, I couldn't wait to hear how "Dr. J" got himself out of this one. God began teaching us to find joy in the moment, and this was just one example of how he did it. His light shined through her, and her strength helped us find ours. Moments like these lightened the heaviness and helped us to shift our focus to what was important.

After several months, Te'ashia's pancreas stopped working altogether making it much easier to control her blood sugars. By the age of 5, I would draw the insulin into the syringe, and she would give herself the shot using an injection device. The doctors told me then that she would likely not see a cure for diabetes in her lifetime; however, in time, medical advancements would no doubt make managing the disease easier.

It was here that I began to learn not to put my confidence in man. Something inside of me told me that the best intentions and the highest level of education and experience couldn't surpass the power and plans of God. So, I asked. I prayed, and I asked for what seemed like the impossible, that my baby would be cured completely of diabetes in her lifetime and I believed with my whole heart that God was able.

get up and go!

Chapter 3

Significant Severe

I'm not afraid of storms for I'm learning how to sail my ship.
Louisa May Alcott

As Te'ashia grew from a child to an adolescent things went relatively smoothly with managing her diabetes. She did have occasional periods of uncontrolled blood sugars. Those usually occurred with a growth spurt; although, at times there just didn't seem to be any rhyme or reason for them at all. Those times resulted in more injections for her because we had to give correction insulin to bring her blood sugar under control. On one of those occasions, we had just moved to a new town, and we started working with a local pediatric doctor. In addition to a period where we were struggling to manage her blood sugars, there were serious challenges with this doctor.

Our first visit had been for a routine, new patient exam that included fasting blood work. We left with a plan to wait until the results were in to make any major adjustments, so the physician could see what her levels had been over the last three months. During the second visit, her blood sugars were still running high. The doctor looked at her chart and saw a note about a new insulin that he wanted us to try, but no one had called to share this with me. When he checked with his nurse, the insulin hadn't even been called into the pharmacy. Also, he noted adjustments to her dosage that hadn't been discussed with me, because no one called. I don't know if he was frustrated with the situation, or maybe he was just having a bad day. Whatever the case, instead of simply giving me the information and starting the plan that day or taking responsibility for the balls that were dropped in his office, he turned his frustration to me. This doctor even went as far as to say that I wasn't doing what I needed to as a mother. I couldn't believe it! I was so angry and just plain stunned at the audacity and lack of accountability of this doctor!

Without going into detail, I responded by leaving him with a check, a REALITY CHECK and we quickly found a new doctor. Even though I knew what he was saying wasn't true, I allowed those words to penetrate my heart and mind. I didn't realize how they grew roots of doubt, and sometimes shame and guilt until sometime later. It took me a long time to break free from these feelings. When things weren't going well, I began to question whether I was doing everything I needed to as a mother. Then I would become frustrated with myself for entertaining those thoughts.

Te'ashia's new doctor was wonderful, and he helped us maintain tight control of her diabetes. In fact, she was only hospitalized once from the onset of the disease up to her teenage years, and that was for pneumonia. Our life didn't focus on diabetes; instead, I tried very hard to raise her in the knowledge that she had the disease, it didn't have her. I wanted her to know that the only limits or constraints this illness put on

get up and go!

her would be the ones she allowed by not managing it. As a result, this girl did everything. Girl Scouts, basketball, chess club, and swimming. She took my teaching so literally that when we took her little brother to try out for football, the coach was impressed as she tossed the ball to her dad on the sideline. He asked if she wanted a place on the team and she accepted. At the first game of the season, we were in the stands with our video camera ready to capture everything. Then it started to rain, so their dad had to take the camera, which was the size of a mailbox back then and lock it in the car. As soon as he did, the quarterback threw the ball to Te'ashia who caught it and ran it in for a touchdown. We were so excited for her.

Not long after her diagnoses we also made it a point to participate in Camps and JDRF events (Juvenile Diabetes Research Federation). These events raised awareness of the disease and funding for research. This kind of activity helped her to see that she was not the only one in this battle. Camps, like Camp Little Shot, gave her a chance to make friends and share stories with others her age.

Once Te'ashia hit puberty, which was late for her, things began to change. Keeping her blood sugars under control with all the hormonal changes was tough enough. Added to that were mood swings and a natural desire for more independence and space. Unfortunately, the desire for independence came without wanting to take full ownership of managing the disease. I would back off the responsibilities, so she could manage them, and when she didn't, I would pick up the reins again. She would resist and say, "I've got it, mom, I don't need your help," and I would step back again. Te'ashia did well for a few weeks then she would stumble. We lived in a full-blown tug of war. We would argue, and her doctors and I would share everything that could and would go wrong if her diabetes wasn't controlled, including blindness, loss of limbs, and renal failure. In the heat of our discussions, I would always say, "I am not giving up a kidney just because you're stubborn or irresponsible," even though I knew that I couldn't back up those words.

We worked so hard to manage this disease throughout her childhood, and she played a huge part in that. Now, stepping into adolescence, it all seemed to be falling apart. I couldn't believe the irresponsible behaviors she was exhibiting. The periods of rarely, if ever checking her sugars, often ignoring levels until they skyrocketed, and at times not giving herself shots. Even when the insulin pump was introduced in her mid-teen years, she would "forget" to bolus (give herself a dose of insulin through the pump) for snacks, and even meals sometimes. You couldn't tell on the outside, but on the inside, I was in a constant state of

get up and go!

combined frustration, worry, anger and sadness, after all, her life was on the line.

With all of this, the reality was that I wasn't the only one who was feeling frustrated, worried, angry and sad. My beautiful, funny, loving teen was having a tough time dealing the demands of diabetes. Pricking her finger for a decade to check her blood sugar multiple times a day and then counting her carbs and programming her pump may not have seemed like a big deal to us, but to her it was. She wanted to be free from diabetes so badly that, at times, she would free herself, even if it was only until she got sick. Skipping insulin doses and bypassing a healthy diet altogether was her way of denying that diabetes existed. By her late teens, these choices landed her in the ICU with a serious complication of diabetes called diabetic ketoacidosis. Ketoacidosis occurs when your blood sugars skyrocket for a period, and your body produces elevated levels of blood acids called ketones. The cost for those brief periods of freedom was high, she almost died.

It was a brief wakeup call for her, and for a while, she managed diabetes so well that her blood sugars were in tight control again. Then, in time, she would slip back into old patterns. Looking back, I can only imagine how difficult it was for her. I think of the many times I've set out to live a healthier lifestyle and incorporate regular workouts. I'd start, do well for a while, but then somewhere along the way, fall off the wagon. She stumbled too, often. People, including me, would tell her, "You just have to be more disciplined." Everyone in her diabetes world SEEMED to have perfect levels. No one was being real about how difficult it was, which I believe is one of the reasons she began to withdraw into a lonely world for a period. The truth is that many people struggle with managing the disease, most just don't feel that they can be honest about it. As a parent, I wasn't open about my struggles or stumbles as I tried to help her. That doctor's words would creep to the surface each time I was about to share, and I was torn between being her protector and shame and guilt. I didn't let those emotions stop me from trying to help her, but I was handcuffed from fighting openly.

Managing her diabetes wasn't the only struggle she faced. It was around the children's teen years that their father and I divorced, and he moved to another state. This was difficult for all my children, and each of them responded differently. In some ways, my sons are still working through underlying remnants of the pain. We all went to counseling, which didn't seem to be effective for my children at the time. A few years later, I

get up and go!

met and married the man God created just for me and I met my two bonus children. Although the two of us were solid, the blending of our families initially came with its own inclement weather. Around this time, behavioral changes that we started to pick up on during Te'ashia's late childhood also become increasingly apparent. For example, her love for reading become a complete fixation with books. As a result, she would sit and read the same series of books over and over, and she would write out lists of other series that she had read or wanted to read. She would do the same with music and movies. In her late teens years, she could tell you the names of the actors and actresses and details for any movie that was within her realm of interest. Te'ashia also started wanting to wear only jeans and a t-shirt, and she only wanted to wear the same clothing brands all the time. She began to withdraw from friends saying that she felt different and she began communicating differently. However; if you were able to get her to talk about a favorite topic, she would go on for days, but she started to find it difficult to talk about a range of topics. She also began to find it hard to follow general instructions. For example, she struggled if you said, I need you to clean the bathroom instead of saying, I need you to wash the tub, clean the sink, and sweep the floor. She needed a list to follow. Te'ashia also began having trouble reading non-verbal cues, things like body language or tone of voice. As a result, she found it difficult to understand when someone was using sarcasm or humor. When her grandfather passed away, who she adored, I remember her seeming unemotional. Everyone deals with grief differently, but this was unusual for her. At the funeral she said, shouldn't I be crying? She saw her grandmother trying to hold it all together from across the room, and she said, "I think I should go and be with her," almost as if she was asking a question instead of making a statement.

We saw several counselors and psychiatrists concerning her father and feelings about diabetes over the years, but no one mentioned anything that stood out. Our communication with her had become strained, and I prayed for understanding and guidance. I had begun researching Asperger's the year before thinking that my nephew may need to be tested. Having remarried a few years after my divorce, my husband and I were talking through the symptoms of Asperger's one day, and he said, "Has Te'ashia been tested?" It hit me like a ton of bricks. I was so focused on helping my nephew that I hadn't considered how the symptoms related to my daughter. That twinge of guilt from years ago also crept back up to the surface. How could I have missed this? My husband quickly shut that thought down. He said, "you have been taking her to

get up and go!

professionals for years seeking their help, and they missed it. The time for you to find out was now. It wasn't intended to be revealed then. I won't let you beat yourself up; you're an amazing mom." After a series of testings, she was diagnosed with high functioning Autism Spectrum Disorder. For us, it opened a world of better communication and more understanding and appreciation for differences. It also helped all of us adjust our expectations and approaches to help bring out the best in one another.

In time I came to learn how sharing your story and addressing things openly, when you are led to do so, releases you from bondage and helps other people. Sure, there are always going to be people who will judge you and criticize your choices, but there is also a freedom in confronting your reality and connecting with others who are bold enough or frustrated enough to confront their own. There is a freedom in saying, I don't have all the answers, I don't always get it right, and that's ok. There is a freedom in granting your child, young or old, this same liberty. Whatever your child is dealing with, rebellion, drugs, depression, self-esteem issues or anything else, I've learned that blaming, shaming, scolding, or self-righteousness never helps the situation. What does help is finding common ground and loving unconditionally. I have in no way mastered this. I was raised in the, "because I said so" and "what goes on in this house, stays in this house" era and I sometimes revert to old habits. I also tend to try to fix or control the situation. I like to call things like these Tyila-isms. When I can move past my isms and make a sincere effort to connect heart to heart with whichever child I am dealing with at the time at the time, I make progress. When we remember that we're on the same team, any walls that have started to build between us begin to crumble. Finding common ground and loving unconditionally doesn't mean that you won't be concerned or that you will always agree with your loved one's choices. It doesn't mean that you will bail them out of repeated poor choices. It's important for them to know that every choice has a consequence and the better their choices, the better the outcome. And in no way does it mean that you will allow any poor decisions to disrupt your household, which is especially important for adult children. There may come a time when you must love an adult child from a distance until they are ready to confront their issues head-on.

What this does mean is that you are willing and ready to love the way God loves us. God loves us unconditionally, but He also cares deeply about what we do, what we say, and how we view ourselves. Through His word, He shows us the right path and gives us the space to choose our own. When we don't follow His plan, He gives us the room to reap the

get up and go!

consequences of our choices while consistently reaffirming and reassuring us of His love over and over again. Proverbs 1:31, ESV tells us "therefore they shall eat the fruit of their way, and have their fill of their own devices." God also lets us know that He delights in nothing more than connecting with us. We often step away from God or allow people and things to come between us, but He is always right there, waiting to reconnect without judgment or condemnation when we choose Him.

All in all, our journey through Te'ashia's teen years looked a lot like her blood sugar levels, some well-managed, some extreme highs, and a few lows covered with lessons learned and a whole lot of grace and mercy.

get up and go!

Chapter 4

Dancing in the Rain

Life isn't about waiting for the storm to pass; it's about dancing in the rain.
Author Unknown

As our children grew, we enjoyed graduations, weddings, and the priceless addition of healthy grandchildren. We also welcomed our littlest lamb, Josiah, home. Family trips, outings, and activities were a normal part of our routine. We even opened a restaurant and at one time or another, all the kids, accept the baby worked there. Our family still laughs at the stories from that adventure while sharing memories and treasuring the people we met. We also watched as our older children stepped out on their own, stretched their wings and practiced applying the lessons they had gained over the years. A couple of them seemed to completely forget all that they had learned, choosing the rockiest roads possible instead. As a result, we received more lessons on keeping our hands out of it and choking down advice unless asked for it. Boy, that's still a tough one for me. I also had to learn not take their poor choices as a blow to our parenting skills. Instead, we just need to be positioned to lovingly encourage them as they take responsibility for their choices, learn from them and fail forward.

Our family experienced hills and valleys like any other family; although, at times it felt like we hung out in the valley a little more than most. And at times we went through more than one storm at the same time. In fact, our son James' accident took place just as our daughter began to experience serious complications with her health. To top it off our youngest son began having challenges at school just before Te'ashia's biggest storm hit.

It was around this time that Te'ashia confided in me that her high school years were a lonely time for her. She had segregated herself from most of her friends and focused on her books. She did make new friends when she began working and when she started college. Te'ashia wanted to move out on her own after finishing school, but by then her body had begun to be impacted by the long-term effects of diabetes coupled with periods of uncontrolled blood sugars. By the time she was 27, Te'ashia's diagnoses had included Neuropathy (nerve damage that caused weakness, numbness, and pain in her legs) and Gastroparesis (also caused by nerve damage and resulting in food not moving as it should from the stomach to the intestines). She also had Macular Edema (the buildup of fluid in the center of the retina) she had a detached retina. She fought these diseases while still working to manage her diabetes and asthma. Next, she began to gain weight very quickly. She went from 130 pounds to over 200 in a matter of months. We went back and forth between her doctors who performed several tests until they discovered the source of the problem,

get up and go!

end-stage renal failure. Soon, in addition to the treatments to correct or control the other diseases, she was on peritoneal dialysis. Peritonea is a form of dialysis that she was able to perform at home. The cycle ran while she slept. Once the dialysis began to pull some of the excess fluid off her, she began to feel better, and her weight remained around 170.

Now she juggled the diabetic, gastroparesis and renal diets as her lifestyle became more complicated and confining than ever before. It was a tough time. It was difficult for her physically, emotionally, and sometimes spiritually as she confided in me that she sometimes asked God what her purpose was.

It was also difficult as a parent to see her go through so much and as a caregiver to balance my load. The family stepped in where they could, although I was the leader of our caregiver team. I was most familiar with her doctors and care plans, and I am mom. There isn't a magic age when you stop being there for your family, no matter how old they are. Looking back, I reminisce about all those wonderful years that we enjoyed managing her care at home without the need for the ER visits or hospital stays that were now far too common. So many times, I would spend most of the night in the ER or up to help her through a tough night, then I would get up the next day and head to work. I would only call out when she was admitted or when the ER visit lasted nearly all night leaving me completely exhausted. I would work until late at night to make up for time missed during the many appointments leaving little time for rest or workouts to relieve stress. I would get it in as best I could and work to rely on God to help me manage it all for a few reasons. First, I needed sources of normalcy to keep me balanced. I enjoyed my job and my work family; it challenged me and gave me an outlet to contribute in many ways. I worked with a supportive leader, peers, and employees and I tried hard to be a supportive leader. While I didn't go in every day sharing our story and I didn't confide in everyone, when God put it on my heart to do so I opened. Many people that I work with had no idea we were going through such a storm, not because I was hiding it, but because that's not how we fight our battles.

I know from experience that opening without being led by God to do so can open the door for negative emotions to come in. People often have good intentions, but their words can sometimes have an adverse effect. I have learned to be cautious about who I share my storms with even in my own family. At one point in this journey, I knew I couldn't share with my mother. She was still processing her emotions about the battle that her oldest grandchild was fighting and became upset anytime I began

get up and go!

to share details. At one point she called me just as I had received some difficult news. I was still processing it, and I was crying. Typically, that's what I do, I cry, I fuss and have a word with God, and I put on my big girl panties and fight. Well, on this occasion I was still in the crying phase of my process, and I knew not to answer the phone, but I did with the hope that she could just let me vent. Instead, she too started crying, and she began talking about what a tough time my daughter has had and how unfair it was. My mom went on to say how much she hates it that I have such a heavy load and how painful and hard this must be for me. She genuinely needed to vent too, and I let her. It just wasn't what I needed at that moment to keep me strong and focused. This call opened the front door of my spiritual house and pity walked right in. It took me the rest of the day of praying and repeating every scripture I know to clean house and get that emotion out. My daughter and I have our moments, but we don't have time for a pity party. Guess who I learned that from? One of the strongest women I know...my mom. Later in this journey, she came to spend some time on the front line with me and Te'ashia. After being candid with her about how we process and fight, she too began to apply the skills she freely taught. She genuinely wanted to be there for us but had to work through the pain of watching those she too loved and protected going through a storm that she couldn't take away. That's when I would see my teacher put on her armor, as I had seen her do my whole life long so that this warrior could stand with her daughter and granddaughter.

By this point, Te'ashia had long since agreed to let me help her manage her care and I agreed to support her and not try to take over. We went through the process of being placed on the transplant waiting list. They gave us an idea of what to expect when we received "the call" telling us that we had a potential donor. The transplant clinic said the wait could be 2-3 years. Her nephrologist said some of his patients receive their calls in a month. And with that, we packed our bags, put them by the door, and we waited.

Life didn't stop because we were waiting and God had a way of working out even the little things. Te'ashia often felt lonely at home all day by herself, and this was just around the time that Josiah transitioned to first grade and began to struggle with this move. One of the first activities of the day was a writing assignment, yet he struggled with writing as a result of his occupational needs, and he had a difficult time expressing this as a result of his speech delays. He began to revert to expressing himself behaviorally. He was angry and frustrated, and he made sure everyone knew it. We worked with his teacher, principal, counselor and vice

get up and go!

principal and tried multiple approaches to no avail. Although the team at his school was supportive, their frustration began to show along with ours, and Josiah's confidence and self-esteem plummeted. Prayerfully we realized that this approach to his education was just not a good fit for him. We decided to try homeschooling him for the remainder of the year. That turned out to be the best decision for all of us. Serving as his learning coach gave Te'ashia something meaningful to do during the day. My husband and I worked with him at night and on the weekends. Josiah's confidence and self-esteem turned around quickly as did his grades and the one-on-one time and attention was just what he needed. We still had a lot of work ahead of us, but this was a great start. As he had done his whole life without knowing it, Josiah helped Te'ashia to stay focused and to find her joy. Each when I got home she always had a funny story to share about their day. And still, we waited for the call.

Again, things were not easy, but we were managing one step at a time. After months of waiting, we went to Florida to begin the process of registering for their transplant list. It was here that we were educated on the term "dry run." That's when you receive the call that there is a potential donor, however; when you arrive, the organ is not a match. Some people experience a few of these before receiving their donor organs. I began praying that there would be no dry runs for us.

In addition to Florida, we also had plans to register in Alabama. Our family and friends remained supportive, and we pressed to enjoy the moment and keep it light. We even held a Facebook poll to have our family help us name T's new organs. It was hilarious and a lot of fun for her. They came up with names like Grace and Mercy, Thing One and Thing Two, Sonny and Cher; the list went on and on. In the end, she chose Captain and Tennille.

During this time, Te'ashia had more hospital stays in one year than she had experienced her whole life. On one occasion she developed a rattle in her chest that sounded like congestion and said that she was having a tough time breathing. We went to the doctor who prescribed a new inhaler and antibiotics. Over the next couple days, she put on quite a bit of fluid, and her breathing became more labored. On Saturday morning of that week, she came banging on my door after my husband had left for work. She was struggling to breathe and said the inhaler and nebulizer weren't working. She told me that she was going to sit on the porch to get some fresh air while I called the doctor. A few minutes passed. I don't know what happened during that time, but Te'ashia came back in fully distressed. She could barely gasp the words, "I can't breathe." I told Josiah

get up and go!

to grab his shoes, I grabbed mine and my purse, and we headed out in our pajamas. Te'ashia skin was quickly changing color, and she was clinging to my arm with one hand and struggling to get the window down with the other, hoping to get some air. I was trying hard not to panic, but I knew there was no way she was going to make it to the hospital in time because we live 20 minutes away. I called 911 and asked them to have an ambulance meet me, and I was quickly becoming frustrated that they didn't seem to know any of the landmarks I was mentioning. At this point, Te'ashia was completely hysterical. She was understandably flailing about trying to get air, but it was making matters worse. That's when she squeezed tighter to my arm to get my attention, and she mouthed the words "please help me." Tears burned my cheeks, and for a moment I felt powerless. I was on the verge of complete panic. I remember these words passing through my head, "I have no control of this situation. Whether she lives or dies right now is out of my hands". Then, just as quickly as I received that wake-up call, these words pierced through my brain boldly, clearly, yet peacefully, "NO, I AM NOT IN CONTROL, BUT I LOVE AND TRUST THE ONE WHO IS." As I exhaled, it was as if all the fear and anxiety that I had been carrying left my body and my focus restored. Those words instantly soothed my soul. I reached over and placed my hand on Te'ashia's shoulder and said, "God's got this." She gazed at me with trusting eyes, and my calm helped her release some of her anxiety. Soon she stopped gasping quite so hard. Hearing the words, "ma'am, ma'am," shifted my attention back to the phone and I remembered that there is a fire department near my son's former school. I asked the 911 operator to have the ambulance meet us there. When we arrived the emergency personnel were waiting for us with oxygen, and they treated Te'ashia until the ambulance arrived. At the hospital, we learned that excess fluid had gotten into her lungs and she nearly drowned in her fluid. They were able to remove the excess fluid and stabilize her. For us, it was another miracle, another step, and another lesson learned. And still, we waited for that call.

A couple of months after that scare, Te'ashia was back in the hospital with gastroparesis challenges. Just when we thought she would be released we were told that she needed to stay one more day for observation. The thought of staying longer was a battle for both us, for our entire family. She had been placed on the transplant list one year and two months earlier. We worked hard to focus on and enjoy the moment and thank God for what we had. Still, we were weary. I call this place "the meantime." It's that place between the time you pray a prayer and the time it's answered. When you first start off waiting, you're optimistic like

get up and go!

we were when she was first added to the list. We were so excited, and we waited patiently. Then one month turned into two and before you know it the seasons changed, and it was time to repack the suitcases with winter clothes. Then, it was time to go through the same routine, this time with clothes for the spring. There were also all the doctor's visits, hospital stays, and ambulance trips to the house. Added to this was the daily set up and breaking down of dialysis supplies. We were simply tired.

We were tired of waiting, tired of running, tired of hurting, tired of being tired. We felt like we were drowning and there were times we felt like throwing in the towel. That's just what the enemy wants us to do, especially when we're close to our victory. He wants us to feel like we're drowning when we have made it all the way through the deep, treacherous parts of the journey to shallow water. We learned that this was the time to praise like never before. It's not easy to praise when you're weary, in fact, Hebrews 13:15 tells us, Through Jesus, therefore, let us continually offer to God a sacrifice of praise, the fruit of lips that openly profess His name. No, it's not easy, that's why is called a "sacrifice of praise." It requires us to press beyond what our circumstances look like and be willing to visualize what's on the other side. It's done based on what you know, not what you feel. It's a way of thanking God for what He's doing to make you stronger, how He's using you to help others and for what He's about to do in your life. And that's just what we did. We cried, we laughed, we hoped, and we praised.

get up and go!

Chapter 5

The Call

The greater your storm, the brighter your rainbow.
Author Unknown

I recently heard about a man who waited 17 years for a kidney transplant. I don't know the circumstances around his journey, but my heart was heavy for him. Even though it often felt like we had been waiting years, the time between being added to the active list and receiving our call was a mere 14 months. Specifically, it was 63 weeks and six days. Translated, we felt every one of those 447 days, we endured each of the 10,728 hours, and we held on to God's hand tightly during every one of the 638,620,800 seconds. Then, it came.

Once added to the active list, I began to imagine what it would be like when we got "the call." Where would we be? Would we be together, so I could see her face and watch that beautiful smile form while her dimples pressed deep into her cheeks? Would it be at night? Would I be at church or work? Would I be able to keep my composure well enough to drive? Many possibilities ran through my head countless times. In the end, it was completely different than anything I imagined. One thing I felt certain of was that when we got the call, it would not be a dry run. We would not make the emotional trip all the way to the hospital and learn that the organs were not a good match.

With the news that Te'ashia would be in the hospital for another day, I decided to head home to wash her clothes and get to the pharmacy to pick up her refills. I was at home folding her laundry when she called me. Half of my attention was on repacking her overnight bag and looking for a book she had asked for when she excitedly announced, "Mom, I got the call." To which I said, "What call?" I assure you that in all the times I had envisioned this moment; never did it start out quite like this. As God would have it, none of this part of the story would be anything like I imagined. Te'ashia, surprised by the response I had given, said, "Mom, THE CALL! They have a donor!" Now she had my full attention, and I felt like my heart would burst from my chest. Then her excitement dwindled as she shared the next part. "But they said I can't have these organs because I'm still in the hospital and the risk is too big." I was still trying to process everything, yet I was already jumping into recovery mode. "What, who said you can't have them? What number did they call from? Did you tell them that you are only there to be monitored?" I spit out these, and I'm sure other questions while anxiously pacing the floor. She told me that the transplant coordinator called her to share and withdraw the good news. I immediately called the coordinator to hear firsthand everything that Te'ashia had shared. I tried to plead our case and expressed that she was only there for observation. Still, the coordinator reluctantly insisted that the risk would be too big, and we would have to wait until next time. She

get up and go!

apologized over and over again and was very empathetic, surely hearing my anguish. Then she tried to reassure me by saying, "the good news is this shows that your daughter is at the top of the list."

I hung up the phone laughing and crying hysterically at the same time. I was gasping for air between all of this. If anyone had seen me, they would have surely thought I had lost it. I said out loud, "God really? After all this time? Like, this?" I took a deep breath and paced more, overwhelmed by so many emotions. Then within just a few of minutes, my emotions leveled out, and my breathing calmed. I said, again out loud, "Ok God, I trust your plan, I trust your timing, and I know what I have prayed, what we have prayed. We don't want anyone else's organs; we want ours. We want the ones we have been praying for." With that proclamation, I thanked Him for letting us know, in His way, to get ready because the time was near. That wasn't the only thing God was letting me know. Instead of allowing me to beat myself up over my initial reaction, He was letting me know how much I had grown. It didn't take me days or hours to surrender this to Him and refocus; it was a matter of minutes. And I had such peace about it. I continued to pace at that point as I prayed for the family who just lost their loved one. Next, I called my husband. Still filled with emotion, I relived the entire story with him as I laughed and cried and celebrated my surrender and growth. I could tell that he too needed time to process all of this.

I called our daughter back and shared the news that we were close. If she was disappointed, you couldn't hear it in her voice. I only heard the excitement of being at the top of the list. God has surrounded us with so many warriors to cover us in prayer and encourage us on this journey to include our family, church family, work family, and friends. I wanted them to share in the good news from this day as well, so I sent this text message to those closest to us within these groups:

WE JUST GOT "THE CALL" - unfortunately, we can't have the kidney and pancreas because she is in the hospital. But this lets us know how close we are. Please join me in praying for all of the families involved with this one. What God has for us is for us.

I finished preparing and repacking her overnight bag and headed to Walmart to pick up prescriptions. While waiting for the last refill to finish, I went the electronics section to look for a new charging cable for Te'ashia. That's when her Nephrologist called. After announcing himself, he excitedly said, "Mrs. Cooks, I just received a call that they have a donor

get up and go!

for Te'ashia." I calmly continued searching for the cable and said, "Yes, I spoke with the coordinator as well and learned that we can't have these organs because she is in the hospital, but it's good to know we're close." He said, "No, no, I told them there is no reason to keep her in the hospital." At this point, I stopped what I was doing, and I froze right where I was. He went on to say, "I called the hospital and told them to discharge her, and I told the coordinator that she is coming. Go get her! These are her organs. They are waiting for you!" I dropped everything I was holding and stood silently trying to process what I had just heard. This was it! These were ours after all! It was her Nephrologists' voice that brought me back to my senses. "Mrs. Cooks, are you still there?" I said, "Yes, yes, yes! Ok, thank you so much, I'm going now!"

Again, one of my favorite expressions is Nullius in verba. "Take nobody's word for it." Not taking the word of others and instead, hearing, researching or finding out for myself over the years has served me well. As fond as I am of her doctor, this is one of those things that I just had to hear first-hand. I called the coordinator back, who was just about to call me. She confirmed everything and gave me step-by-step instructions on what to do and where to come. I tried my best to keep my composure as she confirmed. She told me what a blessing it was and how happy she was for our family. Flooded with emotion, I hung up and began to shout, praise, jump up and down and thank God, right in the middle of the electronics section of Walmart. I felt like King David dancing and praising. I might still be there praising had it not been for the short window of time that I had to go back to the house, pick up our suitcases, pick Te'ashia up, and get to Atlanta, a two-hour drive from our house. I did stop to pray for the donor family again, I called my husband, and I sent this message to our friends and loved ones:

OMG, they called me back!!! Her renal doc worked it out with the surgeon!!!! It's ours!!!! If everything is a match, she will be in surgery by tomorrow!!!! They are dismissing her now, so we can make the drive! I'm in Walmart picking up scripts - shouting and crying. Heading to Atlanta to collect our kidney and pancreas. Please cover us in prayer and pray for the family who just lost their loved one!

As I looked back over this text, I kicked myself a little for including the word "If." I was certain once a coordinator gave the ok to come to Atlanta, then the organs would be ours. There would be no dry runs for us. So why did I feel the need to leave an opening for doubt? An opening that

get up and go!

said, just in case God has a different plan. Just in case I speak it and He doesn't do it the way I thought He should or would. Then I told myself, you're human. Add the puzzle piece to the picture and keep it moving, it will make sense when it's supposed to.

With that, I hurried to our house to grab our suitcases and then to the hospital to pick up a very excited Te'ashia. She was sitting in a wheelchair in front of the hospital with her nurse, and I could see that smile before I pulled into the hospital circle to pick her up. It was so surreal to think that we were so close to having our lives change so drastically. The coordinator asked us to try to arrive in Atlanta by 7:00 pm and we hit the road just in time for rush hour traffic. It seemed to take FOREVER to get there, and I could feel God gently trying to calm me. Our family and friends were blowing up our phones the entire way, and Te'ashia was enjoying reading and sharing their messages. We laughed, and we cried as excitement, energy, and love passed from our vehicle through the phone. When we arrived, we were escorted to the transplant floor of the hospital to have labs drawn so the doctors could confirm the match. But we already knew. They also tested and conducted a biopsy on the donor organs to make sure they were healthy. As I went downstairs to grab a bite to eat, I saw a family leaving, and they were distraught, comforting one another. I wondered if our donor was their loved one. How could we possibly ever thank them enough for making this choice? My heart broke for them. We later learned that the organs were flown into the hospital, so that was not the donor family, simply another family in the midst of a storm.

Te'ashia and I were both so overwhelmed with this precious gift. Excitement, anticipation, expectation, joy, sorrow, so many emotions. We learned that her surgery would be the first one in the morning and 6:30 am was the original time we were given. They suggested that we try to sleep. That was funny. It was like we had been in a Canoe Marathon, seemingly rowing for endless miles. Now that we were close to the finish line, someone said, "it's ok, you can stop rowing now." Not a chance! Te'ashia said she was a little nervous but mostly excited. We talked nearly all night about our journey and what things would be like after the transplant. She shared the things she was most excited about doing, where she wanted to go, how she wanted to live on her own and go back to finish those final two semesters of school. We would doze off here and there but only for a short while. I had no intention of texting our family and friends through the night; however, most insisted on receiving a play-by-play. Others picked back up in the morning to check on our progress. At 2:47 am I sent this text after the nurse entered our room:

get up and go!

Just got word that the organs they are healthy, and we are a solid match!!!! Everything is a go for 6:30 am!!!!

When she came into the room, we were like little kids waiting for this confirmation. We knew it, but we wanted to hear it, and when we did, the flood of tears started all over again. At 3:30 am everything became extremely quiet on the floor and as the tears began to flow again, I sent this text:

A 27-year-old journey is coming to an end in just a few hours. This floor is very quiet right now except that music just started coming from the room next to us. The song is, "It's good to Know Jesus," Lol, I can't stop crying. Everyplace I turn is a sign that He's right here and has been all along. She will be the first surgery in the morning. 6:30. Pray. Pray. Pray

The lyrics of the song are:

It's good to know Jesus,
It's good to know Jesus,
(He's the lily of the valley),
(a bright and morning star),
It's good to know the Lord.

I came to Jesus just as I was; I was weary, wounded, and sad;
I've found in Him a resting place
And He has made me glad.
It's good to know Jesus,
It's good to know Jesus,
(He's the lily of the valley),
(a bright and morning star),
It's good to know the Lord.
I love the Lord, He heard my cry,
And He pitied every groan.
'Long as I live while trouble rise,
I'll hasten to His throne.
It's good to know Jesus,
It's good to know Jesus,
(He's the lily of the valley),
(a bright and morning star),
It's good to know the Lord.
It's good to know Him;
It's good to know the Lord.

get up and go!

Oh, it's good to know Him,
It's good to know the Lord.

    The next morning my husband got our two youngest children settled and headed to Atlanta. He wanted to lay eyes on Te'ashia, who he calls baby girl before she went in for surgery and we all wanted to pray together. For months we had prayed over this surgical team, every decision they would make, every detail of this process. Other than being on an emotional high, we were very much at ease and filled to the brim with grief for the donor family. We met the surgical team, and they explained the process, the length of this very long surgery and when we could expect regular updates on their progress. We shared the names of her new organs, and the team got a kick out of it. We prayed together, kissed our daughter goodbye and basked in the moments.

    Everything went like clockwork. The first sign that this transformation was taking place came at 7:34 am when I received an alert from Te'ashia's pump app. This is a pump that also monitored her blood sugar and sent alerts to family members through an app on their phone when there was a high or low level. At that moment a "no signal" alert came to my phone from the device. As tears flowed down my cheeks I sent a picture of the screen to my mom and family on our group text and sent this message:

Momma, check this out!! It's the last time that we are gonna get a signal from her blood sugar monitor!

    The surgery had just begun and I was already trying to figure out how to get the dialysis machine and the dialysis solution that took up a fourth of our daughter's room, out of our home. I didn't want a single remnant of kidney disease or diabetes. I suggested a bonfire, but I knew someone could use the supplies, so I chose alternative routes.

    Then at close to 8:00 am one of the nurses came out to the lobby searching for me. In her hand was a plastic bag containing our daughter's insulin pump. Tears stung my eyes, and I reached for this precious gift. After all this time, it was about to be over. A few hours later we received notice that the pancreas was successfully in and the kidney was next. Then at 2:33 pm I sent this message:

Just spoke with the surgeon, everything went well, and everything's in place. Now we just wait for those babies to make themselves at home and

start working! Thank you so much for standing with us on this very special day!

I wanted to shout from the rooftops and tell the world just how good God is. I placed a picture of Te'ashia being transported to surgery on my Facebook page with these words:

Today, after 27 years of living with Type I Diabetes, our daughter was finally set free. God didn't answer our prayers for healing in our time, and He didn't do it the way we thought He would. No, this journey included years in the valley, physical and emotional pain and sometimes heartache. It included the addition of Renal Failure and over a year of dialysis. It included deferred dreams of living independently, finishing school and sometimes, simply being able to enjoy a regular meal.

As we look back over this sometimes-rocky road, it will be with knowledge of how we've grown along the way. How our faith muscles grew, and we learned to find joy in each moment instead of waiting until we reached the destination. It will include how we learned to love first, forgive each other often, and to extend the grace extended to us by God. And most importantly, it will be a reminder that the real gift is in learning to stay in the presence of God, to praise Him just for who He is and to find joy in Him regardless of our circumstances.

Today, we stand in prayer for the family who is mourning the loss of their loved one, and we thank them for their conscious choice to support organ donation. Today, we say "buh bye" to diabetes and kidney disease. YOU DON'T LIVE HERE ANYMORE!

get up and go!

Chapter 6

Nevertheless

There are some things you learn best in calm, and some in storm.
Willa Cather

After the surgery was complete, we were escorted to her room back on the transplant floor. As we entered, the first thing we saw was her dry erase board. One of her nurses had written, "Welcome to the family Captain and Tennille!" When she opened her eyes, her brother and sister had arrived. She looked up at her brother and said, "I'm not a diabetic anymore!"

Everything went so smoothly the first few days. I hadn't had much sleep, but I promised everyone that I would sleep as soon as this girl peed! That would be our indication that her new kidney was starting to function. Thankfully, her organs were functioning beautifully, and she was doing her part to help the healing process. Although her incision spanned from an inch below her breasts all the way to her lower abdomen, she was sitting up the day after surgery and walking the day after that. By mid-week, she upgraded to a full diet, and that's when the smooth sailing came to an end. I learned that our stomach and intestines naturally have a tough time waking up, so to speak, after a surgery. For those with Gastroparesis, it takes even longer. Te'ashia quickly began to experience some nausea and vomiting. The newly stitched incision made the process even more agonizing. Still, she fought. She wanted to be home for the 4th of July, and by June 30th she was doing better. The surgeons believed her to be well enough to go home. Since we had dealt with the Gastro problems before, managing nausea would hopefully be within our span of control.

When we arrived home, it wasn't to the party that our family would have loved to have given her. To keep Captain and Tennille from rejecting, Te'ashia received medication to ensure that her immune system remained low. This meant that extra precautions had to be taken to limit her exposure to anything that could cause infection. As a result, instead of a party, we had a simple banner that said:

Est. 2017
Welcome Home Captain and Tennille
Live the Life You've Always Dreamed of
Congratulations Te'ashia!

Once released from the hospital we worked hard to get all new medications into an organized system. With the anti-rejection drugs, now it was even more critical not to miss a dose. Things went well Friday and most of Saturday. From then on, nausea and vomiting gradually became more than we could manage. We stayed in close contact with the transplant team and followed their guidance. Monday morning was by far

get up and go!

the worst of it, but thankfully she had a follow-up appointment. When we arrived, she was dehydrated, and her blood pressure was 60/43. She was quickly given IV fluids and re-admitted.

Tuesday was July 4th; we had planned to drive to a spot near the Riverwalk in our small town to watch the fireworks safely away from any crowds of people. She really wanted to celebrate her new independence. Instead, half of our children were able to visit us in the hospital room that we would make our home for nearly the next month. The nurses told her that she had the best view in town. It was amazing. You could see the skyline of the city of Atlanta looking like a miniature canvas on the backdrop of the Hospital's University Campus. We were able to see multiple fireworks shows from her window that night, although she was too sick and too weak to join us at the window. She simply wanted to rest and not feel nauseous or have reflux and stomach pain anymore.

For the next several days the pain, reflux, nausea, and vomiting continued. She was so miserable that nothing the doctor's tried seemed to give her relief for long. It was agonizing to see my child in so much pain, and this had become a far too familiar place for me. This time it seemed to hurt even more because it was on the heels of what we thought was the finish line. We thought it was the beginning of the concluding chapter in the long, drawn-out story. I felt like a soldier in the middle of a fierce battle, standing and protecting my troops, all the while feeling the sting of fiery darts. Darts of fear, doubt, worry, and anger that she would continue to endure even more. As I stepped back and refocused through the pain, I could see a little more clearly. I know my Father, and I began to realize that there was yet something else that He wanted to press out of me, out of us, before this chapter ended.

As we continued, the doctors were concerned; the nurses had so much empathy for her, yet relief did not come. The saving grace in this was that Te'ashia's creatinine level (the level that measures how the kidney is functioning) and blood glucose level both showed that Captain and Tennille were still doing great in their new home.

Thankfully I was able to take a leave of absence to be with Te'ashia. We had our teenager and six-year-old at home and worked hard to try to keep somewhat of a balanced routine for them. The disruption to our already bumpy routine was toughest on our six-year-old, Josiah, who struggled with substantial changes. I had already been gone for most of June with her evaluation in Florida and then the transplant. I had also attended a conference for work in June. My husband and I work full time for the same company. He also serves as the part-time Youth Pastor at our

get up and go!

church where I serve as the Life Groups Pastor. With all of this, our plates were full. My husband brought our sons to the hospital when possible and would occasionally switch places, giving me a break and allowing him time to spend time with our daughter. Unless Te'ashia was really struggling, I would sometimes make the two-hour drive home to visit with the family and return to the hospital the next morning. Our son and daughter-in-love would also help with the younger boys' schedules and make the drive when possible to support their sister. Our son James, who worked two jobs, rearranged his schedule to be there for the family. When I thanked him, he said, "Mom you don't ever have to thank me, it's what we do."

On one occasion when my husband brought our younger sons, MJ and Josiah up for a visit, Josiah asked me if we could go for a walk. I said, "Sure." While we were walking he said, "Mommy, will you go on a date with me." I told him that I would love to go on a date with him. I was thrilled that he even asked, and we made it happen that very week. This little guy opened my doors and everything during our date, behaviors that resulted from being in his daddy's classroom of life. These moments were gifts that I treasured.

After three weeks of battling Gastroparesis and GERD (Gastroesophageal reflux disease), the doctors and GI specialists were able to find a regiment that began easing her vomiting, nausea, pain and discomfort. Three weeks with little nutrition had taken its toll, and she was terribly weak. She had to be assisted to the restroom because without aid it was difficult for her even to lift her head from the pillow. As Gastroparesis and GERD eased out, Te'ashia's creatinine and blood sugar levels began to move past the normal range gradually. So much so that a kidney biopsy was required to rule out rejection. When I heard the news I immediately sent this to my prayer warriors:

Stand with us in prayer family. The doctor just told us that her organs are showing initial signs of rejection. I reject that! We believe God to finish this good thing He has started without interruption! They will do a biopsy soon to learn more. Psalm 62:5-12 says, "Yes, my soul, find rest in God; my hope comes from Him. Truly He is my rock and my salvation; He is my fortress, I will not be shaken".

My husband and I started working toward a new goal in January of this year. Last year my goal was to learn a scripture or passage each month. This year we decided to each choose six for the year and take the same approach to learning one per month. Sometimes we will be in the

get up and go!

car, and one of us will say, "hit me with one," and we'll recite a passage that we've learned. We have found that this helps us to get the Word in our spirit. I often use them to start my prayers, and I use them to stand on what I know and encourage myself. With everything that had taken place over the last few weeks, even though I had my quiet time with God I still hadn't begun to look over this month's passage. I pulled it out the morning of the biopsy and committed it to memory as I drove to Atlanta from home:

Isaiah 46:9-11
Remember the former things, those of long ago; I am God, and there is no other; I am God, and there is none like me. I make known the end from the beginning, from ancient times, what is still to come. I say, 'My purpose will stand, and I will do all that I please.' From the east, I summon a bird of prey; from a far-off land, a man to fulfill my purpose. What I have said, that I will bring about; what I have planned, that I will do.

The power of this passage coursed through my veins. It was a great reminder of the miracles that God had performed in the past, the fact that He wrote this story, and that nothing and no one would change the ending He planned. It also reminded me that there is a purpose for everything and that all things do work together for our good even when it doesn't feel like it or look like it.

When the results came back they showed just what we had declared; there was no rejection. The results did appear to show a condition called TMA (Thrombotic Microangiopathy) which is a rare but serious medical condition. This disease results in damage that can occur in blood vessels most commonly inside the kidney and brain. Microangiopathy meant that blood clots were involved which was thought to be a side effect of one of the anti-rejection meds. There were just a few places on the kidney that seemed to be impacted. Doctors also suspected that the pancreas had been affected which was resulting in a low-grade fever. The anti-rejection drug was immediately changed to an alternative medication. The treatment plan included something called Plasma Exchange. With this process, Te'ashia's plasma would be separated from her blood to remove any diseased substances that might be circulating. Next, her plasma would be replaced with donor plasma. She would go through one treatment per day for the next five days. In addition to this, she was beginning to develop Parkinson like symptoms as a side effect to one of the medicines used to help control the Gastroparesis. The medical team addressed this by replacing that medication as well.

While we celebrated the fact that there was no rejection, God was pressing me for something more. There was something else inside of me, something that He had woven into me when I was yet in my mother's womb (as Psalms 139 tells me). Something that had yet to manifest. He was working to build up a different muscle group inside of me. I began studying the three different versions of the story about the woman with an issue of blood. Matthew 9:20-21:

"And behold, a woman who had suffered a discharge of blood for 12 years, came up behind Him and touched the hem of His garment. For she said to herself, "If I only touch His garment, I will be made well."

Those words touched my aching soul. I longed for my baby to receive the healing from her issue of blood that this woman received. I felt like I was not only touching the hem of His garment, I was clinging to it. I was fighting to stand strong for her and intercede where she was weak. What else was needed? Why was this happening? Was I carrying any doubt, not believing enough? What was God trying to teach me from the story?

As I reread the verse over and over, searching for what I was intended to get out of it, it felt like a weight was added to the barbell of this lesson in God's gym of life. No doubt, it was intended to strengthen my faith muscles, but how? Then I started to see something else in "this touch." Years ago, I started an interior decorating business with a friend. We had several planning sessions to prepare for this venture. During our last session, just before we headed downtown to purchase our business license, we jokingly shook hands. Even though this was a lighthearted gesture, this touch of our hands signified our commitment and agreement to the decision that we would enter this business relationship. At that moment I knew that God was pressing me to touch and agree with Him, to commit, to completely be in one accord with His plans for our daughter. Plans that I could not fully see. He had entrusted me to be her mother, and He wanted me to trust Him, the one who loved her more than I ever could, with this part of her story no matter the outcome.

I continued to process this as the weight of these thoughts began to penetrate my being. I began to feel a release as I *started* letting go of things I didn't realize that I was holding. It was painful to face my thoughts and fears. It was difficult to begin letting go of those things I "thought" I controlled. And just the mere thought of trusting God "no matter the outcome," was very unsettling, to say the least. I was pressing into God to

get up and go!

get everything out of this lesson that He intended. Although, I must admit that there are times that I wanted to say, "God, just this once, can I get the Cliff Notes version instead of going through the whole lesson."

As a veteran warrior on God's battlefield, I knew that I needed to call on other warriors that He has placed in my life to stand with me and help me press through this part of the journey. They would cover me as I went in for battle. For months my husband, who I routinely call first, had been planning a beach trip for the teens in our church. Even though we had plenty of chaperones, I encouraged him to go as planned. I knew this time with the teens would be good for them and it would be a good diversion for him. As my best friend, I share everything with him. We stand together and grow together in every aspect of our lives. I am so grateful for him. Whenever something happens, good, funny, sad, whatever, we can't wait to share it with one another. Once, I even called him, and before I caught myself, I said, "girl, you're not gonna believe this." He laughed and said, "You just took our relationship to a new level."

This whole thing was weighing heavily on my husband. Because God made us such unique creatures and He has a different purpose for each of us to fulfill, He uses different experiences to strengthen different faith muscles in each of His children. Mine were strong in some of the areas that were strained in my husband and vice versa. At this part of our journey, God was pressing something out of him as well, yet it was in many ways different than what would be strengthened in me. I was sensitive to this and knew that if I shared this part of my workout with him at this moment, it might come across filled with emotion. Also, if God had not yet helped him work through this part, it could add to the burden he was working to release.

Instead, God put on my heart two people who he wanted me to reach out to, my aunt and one of my friends. My aunt entered a relationship with God in her twenties; she has been my mentor for most of my life, whether she always knew it or not. She is a mighty veteran warrior, and she has also stood with me in this storm, moment by moment, play by play. The friend he put on my heart is also a warrior. Like my journey, God has used her past experiences and choices to transform her into one of His strongest and most faithful daughters. I called my aunt first and tearfully expressed what God was pressing out of me. I told her about what I thought He was asking of me, to come into total agreement with Him whatever His plan may be, and that it was peaceful yet painful. Peaceful because it would be a total surrender to Him and that is just what I needed. Painful, because that meant trusting Him even if it meant that my

get up and go!

daughter's healing might be the ultimate healing. It would mean that the rest and healing of her body may take place in heaven instead of on earth. The abundant life that we hoped and prayed that she would experience may be directly in His arms instead of mine.

My aunt listened, before speaking. When she spoke, I heard in her voice that she had taken on some of my pain. I knew if my aunt could take this all away and carry the burden she would, but we both knew that for whatever purpose, whatever plan God was working to fulfill, this must be. After a few moments, my aunt saturated me with prayer and our tears flowed together. Then, the sadness and heartbreak in her voice began to sound firm and strong. I had heard this shift many times before and felt it coming from my mouth. It's the place where He who lives inside of you gives you strength that is not your own strength. God's spirit that dwells in you gives you the courage and boldness to stand on His word and to declare it.

Exodus 17 tells of a great battle in which the Israelites were encountering their first opposition while wandering in the desert. The Amalekites, a group of raiders, attacked the people of Israel. While Joshua led the troops into battle, Moses, along with Aaron and Hur, watched the battle from a nearby hill. Exodus 17:11 reads, "So it came about when Moses held his hand up, that Israel prevailed, and when he let his hand down, Amalek prevailed." Eventually, Moses became weary, and so Aaron and Hur responded by holding up his arms until the Israelites were able to defeat the Amalekites finally.

Equipped with this battle in mind she firmly and boldly said, "I don't know why God is doing this, and I don't know how anything good will come from it, but I trust God, and I know it will. You are like Moses standing on the hill with your arms up fighting for victory. When you become weary I am standing, I will hold your arms up for you just like Aaron did and your cousin, her daughter and another of the warriors in my circle, will be on the other side like Hur." That image immediately pressed into my mind and gave me strength that would grow stronger in the days to come.

Next, I called my friend who also listened before speaking. Then she prayed a thunderous prayer over me, covering me. After praying, she said, "I need to tell you what God has put on my heart. As a mother, you have taken Te'ashia as far as you can. You have walked her up to the finish line, but you can't make her crossover because this is her fight, and she must want it. You can stand with her, encourage her, and love her, but you must leave room for her to seek God for herself. There are some things

get up and go!

that He wants her to get from this that are intimate and only between the two of them.

I immediately knew she was right. A couple of days before God had begun to show me this very thing when our son James called me. He said, "Mom I need you to do something for me. On Te'ashia's whiteboard write 'I am healthy' and tell her to say it to herself several times a day. I was overwhelmed that my son, who I knew was still working on areas of his relationship with God, had hit the nail on the head. Whether he fully realized it or not, these words were life. My mind went to these Proverbs: *Proverbs 18:21 Death and life are in the power of the tongue, and those who love it will eat its fruits. And Proverbs 23:7 for as He thinks in His heart, so is He.*

Especially in her weakness, what she spoke and what she believed would be her declaration. I couldn't do this for her. I sent a picture of what I had written on the board to our son. To which he said, "No mom, I need it to be in all caps." I wanted to roll my eyes at his critique, but I knew he was right. After all; this was a declaration.

Once I had completed these calls, I sat and prayed again. Both women God put on my heart covered me in prayer and gave other tools for this journey. I am very careful in saying that they both listened before they spoke. It wasn't just my voice they were listening for. They were waiting to hear from God to make sure what they spoke was from Him and not their thoughts on what should be said. They didn't try to talk me out of this process or make me feel as if I was simply doubting God and needed to exercise more faith. They didn't try to encourage me with blanket scriptures or empty words, they stopped, and they listened...then they spoke. Their words aligned with what God had already begun to introduce to me. Their stance reinforced my own. Later in the day when I shared all of this with my husband, I knew it was the right time. We cried together, and we prayed together.

I went back to the room and spoke with our daughter who was only getting up to use the restroom at this point. I was very candid with her about where her health was at this point, and I told her that this fight was hers. She would have to seek God for herself to discover His plans for her life. She would also have to do her part to eat, walk, drink and take her meds if she wanted to win this battle. Te'ashia looked surprised by my candor, but her response let me know that she understood.

During this time, I kept a diffuser in her room and added lavender essential oils to it during the evening which kept her room calm and helped her rest. I used other recipes for nausea and activity, like peppermint,

get up and go!

grapefruit, and lemon. The medical staff often joked that this was their favorite room and mentioned how relaxing it was. While she soaked in all that I said, I added some peppermint to the diffuser. Soon after, she said, "I'm ready to take a shower and then can we go for a walk." She started out walking around the hall once or twice. Over the course of the next couple of days, she began wanting to walk outside. At first, we took the wheelchair for when her strength began to diminish. Soon she was taking long walks outside of the hospital without the chair.

To try to keep a balance at home, when possible I continued to make the trip to our home. Because she experienced such difficult nights, I often slept on a chair in her room. Eventually, I brought the air mattress back in that we used when she initially received her transplant. At the beginning of our journey, we learned from other long-term families how handy it would become. Friends offered us places to stay, and we could have gotten a room, but when your loved one is going through the tough nights that she went through, you want to be there to support them. One morning, about three days after our talk, I came in to find that she had added more words to her board. In addition to, 'I am healthy,' she now had, 'I am healed' and 'I am a daughter of the King.' In all caps of course.

Things seemed to be turning around in some areas, while in others, like her hemoglobin levels and her kidney function, they did not. She continued to need blood transfusions every 2 to 3 days, and her creatine levels continue to climb higher which was an indication that the kidney function was worsening. On top of this, she began to retain fluid again and this had not happened since before the transplant. The doctors planned another biopsy, suggesting again that her organs may be rejecting. This time they planned to sedate her to make the procedure easier on her.

After the procedure, her doctor stood in the doorway of her room updating me on how things had gone. During our conversation, he received a call and excused himself as he turned slightly. The patient they were discussing had taken a turn. Fluid and blood had gotten into their lungs impacting their oxygen level. Their blood pressure was climbing, and they were anxious about not being able to breathe. The doctor said that this person needed to be placed in ICU, then he said, "Yes I'll notify the family, in fact, I'm with her mother now."

You just can't make this stuff up. It's like you're running a race and each time you get to the finish line, the rules change, and you're told you must run one more lap. I was escorted down to the ICU so that I could see her. The ICU at the hospital was like nothing I had ever seen before. Imagine a huge circle with two circles in it. Right in the middle, the inner

get up and go!

circle was the nurse's station. A wall separated it from the next circle. It was divided into several patient rooms that could be accessed from the nurse's station. It could also be accessed from the third and outer circle. The outer circle was a long, round hallway. The entrance to each patient's door was on one side and long windows covered the other side. The door into every room was divided by a partition on each side. Two chairs were placed outside of each door for family members. The hallway was about 5 feet wide, making for a very narrow walkway. Te'ashia's room was all the way around at the end of the circle. As I walked around the circle toward her room, I could see and feel the pain on the faces of other family members. I tried hard not to be so consumed with our journey that I missed seeing a small path connecting us to one of these families. Even if we were only intended to take a couple of steps with them, I wanted to be ready. God taught me this lesson a few years back when I sent an accolade to another employee at our company. I wanted to recognize and thank him for always being so helpful to our department. When this person received it, he sent me an email. It was one of the most impactful thank you messages that I had ever received because it contained these five words, "thank you for seeing me." The thought that there are people who walk on this earth feeling like they are not seen broke my heart, although I knew it to be true and sometimes felt it in my youth. Then I asked myself, as a leader, a pastor, a human being and most importantly a child of God, how many times had I missed seeing someone. Do I get so caught up in my activities for the day, my "to do" list, my agenda, and my journey, that I miss seeing those He intends for me to see? Do I miss hearing Him as He guides me to pray or stand with them? I knew the answer was yes, and I knew this lesson was intended to make me more aware. As I walked those hallways while she was in ICU, I could at times, sense God urging me to connect with others. Sometimes it was simply to share a smile, other times it was a word of encouragement or prayer, and sometimes it was just to be an ear. It was important to know the difference because only God knew exactly what spiritual medicine was needed and in what dosage.

Our family and friends consistently continued to send words of encouragement. They prayed with us, sent gas cards and pre-cooked frozen meals. One of my sister-friends and her fiancé drove over 5 hours to come and visit us for 2 hours and drive back. Our pastor and former pastor and their wives visited at different times. Each came to do and say as God had guided them. We were so grateful for those God sent to stand with us. I've heard many "church folks" complain that no one was there for them when they went through their tests and trials. During this time in our lives

get up and go!

when I was thanking God for His grace and the circle of warriors encamped around us, He reminded me that, in part, "we have this" because "we are this." We are reaping the harvest of seeds that we planted so many times before when others were going through their storms. We have been the love and the support that we have received, not out of expectation or to gain anything in return; it's just who God created us to be. I humbly received this reminder.

Soon after Te'ashia was stabilized, we received the results of the second biopsy; results that were like having a tsunami hit your homeland just after an earthquake. The diagnosis of TMA was the earthquake. We were now learning that the cause of the TMA was HUS, Hemolytic Uremic Syndrome. The treatment and prognosis, we quickly learned, were straightforward, unless you had *Atypical* HUS. This type of HUS is so rare that it only occurs in about 2 out of every 1 million people. Guess what? Yes, you guessed it.

Further testing confirmed AHUS (Atypical Hemolytic Uremic Syndrome). It is a life-threatening disease that can progress quickly and one that often has a genetic component. As I understand it, this syndrome is caused by a problem with the immune system triggered by the side effect of the anti-rejection medicine. Typically, when our bodies are exposed to bacteria or anything foreign, the complement system branch of the immune system will turn on like a light switch and work to destroy the foreign matter. Once the matter is destroyed, the light switch turns off, unless you have AHUS. In this case, the switch stays on, and a system that is intended to fight against the harmful stuff begins to fight the good and cause destruction. Often the kidneys, digestive system, heart, and brain are impacted. The prognosis was once 79% fatal until the VERY expensive immunosuppressive drug called Eculizumab, also known as Solaris, was approved as a treatment option. Why do I know all of this? Because even though I was overwhelmed by the winds and debris, I was in fight mode. Each evening, once our daughter was able to get enough relief from the pain and vomiting to slip into a couple of hours of sleep, I studied. I looked up every term, and studied every diagnosis, and looked through sources and resources so that by the next morning when the doctors made their rounds, I could be her advocate. It allowed me to ask good questions and serve as a strong voice in her weakness. I intended to be a partner in her care plan and not blindly follow anyone down a path that so few had embarked. The hospital care team seemed supportive of, encouraging my involvement and considered my recommendations. If they were frustrated with my lists of questions or our family and theirs, they didn't let it show. I

get up and go!

plainly asked that they always be transparent with me and let me know if I needed to allow more space for them to do their job and I intended to be transparent as well.

I had to press for quiet moments, moments that my mind wasn't running to process all of this or just running ahead to the next step. As I did, some of my prayers came from low places, and I fought to keep my focus. I fought to stand on what I know and not what I felt. I was searching for answers, trying to figure all of this out and fighting to agree with God. During one of these battles He brought back to my remembrance two other verses:

Luke 5:12
While Jesus was in one of the towns, a man came along who was covered with leprosy. When he saw Jesus, he fell with his face to the ground and begged Him, "Lord, if you are willing, you can make me clean.

And Luke: 22:42 Father, if you are willing, take this cup from me; yet not my will, but yours be done."

I read and reread these passages, believing they were the important pieces of the puzzle that I had been waiting for. Just as the man was covered with leprosy, I was covered with the weight of the events leading up to this point. And even though I believed that I was in agreement with God's plan, there was still some shred of control that I was still holding. The cup that I held in my hands seemed so insignificant compared to the one that Jesus held, yet the pain of witnessing flesh of my flesh and blood of my blood endure so much brought me to my knees. The pressure built up, and just when I thought I would boil over...I surrendered. With tears pouring down my face I spoke this prayer, this passage wi+h ~~ emphasis that I had never uttered before. I said, "God if you are willi heal her, I know you can. I believe it with everything in my being. Nevertheless, not my will but yours be done."

As those familiar words left my mouth, this time in full surre envision the old teapot my mother used to keep on her stove. Just as she would pull the lever back to release the steam from the boiling pot, my surrender released the pressure from me.

get up and go!

Chapter 7

Completion

The enemy said, "You can't withstand the storm." The warrior said, "I am the storm."
Author Unknown

My complete surrender didn't end the process that we had to go through with this storm. The severity of this storm was the kind that I had ministered and prayed with others about as they went through battles of their own. Could I practice what I preached when I found myself under the kind of pressure that so many I have counseled over the years had endured? Now that I was held to the flame in a new way, one that tested my faith from every angle, would I remain faithful, would I remain at peace? Would I keep my eyes on God? Could I praise Him, even in the deepest, darkest crevices of the valley?

The day after my full surrender, all these thoughts ran through my head, and I was exhausted from the final relinquishing of control, control that I never had to begin with. I reflected on how bodies resemble a house. The body is the frame of the house, and it consists of our speech, senses, and actions. Within the walls of our body is our soul that consists of our mind, heart, and will. At the center of the house is our spirit and if we are believers, God's spirit, the Holy Spirit. Just like in our physical house, if we are not careful, we can leave a door or window open and unwanted pestilence can enter our house. The same is true with what we watch, listen to and engage in. They can allow things into our spiritual house that were never intended to be there. I think of those who live in areas that routinely have severe weather like a beach house. When a storm is forecasted, homeowners take extra precautions to protect their dwelling from inclement weather like boarding up windows. We also naturally take steps to prevent thieves from entering, things like alarm systems, cameras and other devices to keep our home safe. Over the years I have found that similar precautions are needed to protect my spiritual house from becoming vulnerable. Spending time with God through prayer and study is my way of boarding up my windows and adding an alarm system. It has helped me to keep my mind strong and focused both in and out of the storms. Having a thankful heart in good times and bad has helped me to be on guard against the ultimate thief, Satan, who would like nothing more than to destroy me and my house. Still, at that moment I felt like I had exhausted all my energy, physical and mental resources. As I opened my eyes that morning, the thought of getting up to face another day seemed like too much. My house seemed vulnerable. The mere thought of going back into battle, watching my child endure more felt like a huge boulder laying on my chest, making it difficult for me to breath.

After her release from ICU, our daughter once again occupied the room she recovered in after the transplant. This time it looked, small, dark

get up and go!

and gloomy. In comparison to her other room, the one we had just spent a month in, it was. This space along with the pain she was feeling, both physically and mentally were taking a toll on her. She was losing her fight again. Her precious mind and heart were heavy from the battle, one that never seemed to end, and it broke my heart.

As I laid there on the air mattress, forcing the air to enter and leave my lungs, I prayed. Then, with hot tears rolling down my face, I was silent. That's when God shifted my mind to the first chapter of Joshua, one of my favorite chapters.

"After the death of Moses, the servant of the Lord, the Lord said to Joshua the son of Nun, Moses' assistant, "Moses my servant is dead. Now therefore arise, go over this Jordan, you and all this people, into the land that I am giving to them, to the people of Israel."

God's words stuck in my mind, "Arise, go." This wasn't a suggestion; it wasn't a request. This was a command. As I replayed the passage repeatedly in my mind, I began to draw strength from it. It reminded me of the many times I had told my children to do something that they were reluctant to do. Even though they didn't want to do it, I knew that it was for a greater good, often for their good. The message was clear, **get up and go!** I didn't want to do it. I wanted to pull the covers over my head, but I knew I would drown in pity, so I pressed on. Soon this command spread from my mind to my heart, to my will. And I began to move. I can imagine the devil looking on saying, oh no, here she goes again. He got her to get up!

I grabbed my iPad and left the room, so I could have some serious one-on-one time with God. I made my way outside where I played music, praised, prayed, and cried, all right there on a bench on the Hospital's University Campus. When I finished, I felt a renewed strength, courage, and boldness. It was no longer my strength and energy that I was relying on. It was God's. I read the rest of the first chapter of Joshua, and I was filled with expectation and promise.

"Every place that the sole of your foot will tread upon I have given to you, just as I promised to Moses. From the wilderness and this Lebanon as far as the great river, the river Euphrates, all the land of the Hittites to the Great Sea toward the going down of the sun shall be your territory. No man shall be able to stand before you all the days of your life. Just as I was with Moses, so I will be with you. I will not leave you or forsake you. Be strong and courageous, for you shall cause this people to inherit the land that I swore to their fathers to give them. Only be strong and very courageous, being careful to do according to all the law that Moses my

get up and go!

servant commanded you. Do not turn from it to the right hand or to the left, that you may have good success wherever you go. This Book of the Law shall not depart from your mouth, but you shall meditate on it day and night, so that you may be careful to do according to all that is written in it. For then you will make your way prosperous, and then you will have good success. Have I not commanded you? Be strong and courageous. Do not be frightened, and do not be dismayed, for the Lord your God is with you wherever you go."

I didn't know who all I was leading, but I was certain that the first step was for me to move my feet. There was something in our storm that would help another with theirs. God helped me begin to see this storm more clearly than I ever had.

I thought back to the people I had encountered during both storms we faced with our children. In waiting rooms, chapels, hallways, cafeteria's, those who I or someone in my family ministered to, prayed for and prayed with. If we had not been there, we never could have done those things. We have crossed paths with so many people over the years and just to think for one moment that any part of our story could help them through theirs was a gift. It reminded me of a person I prayed with while in the ICU. The woman was heavy, not knowing if her husband would make it through the night. We prayed and talked together. We spoke and offered encouragement to one another in the days that followed. And then, after we moved out of ICU, I didn't see her again. As with many of the people that I prayed with, I often wondered what God's plan was for their life. This time, He let me see it. Two weeks after we left ICU, as I was returning to the hospital after a visit home. I stepped into the elevator and there she was. She was beaming with excitement and shared with me that she was going to get the car, her husband was well and was being discharged. God used examples like these to help me to see that there was so much purpose in our pain. Purpose that we will never fully know, but when we trust Him to do the leading, we will share some of our hope with someone who has none. We will share our God with someone who doesn't know Him for themselves.

As I examined my house for cracks or crevices, I noticed that I had let some bitterness in. My faith had been stretched to capacity, no doubt and some emotions had gone without being confronted which allowed a bitter root to start growing in the garden of my heart. When my physical house begins to feel cluttered, I turn to an approach that a friend taught me. I get the biggest box I can find and put it in one of the rooms in my house. Starting on the first day of the month, I begin selecting items I am

get up and go!

not using or that no longer fit. I include things that don't fit my physical body and those that no longer fit where I am in life. Whatever date I'm on, I add that number of items to the box. For example, on the first day, I add one item, on the second day I add two. By the end of the month, I have purged 465 items from my house. I recycle them, sell them or take them to Goodwill. The same is true with my spiritual house. I must declutter from time. If it has to do with a person or emotion that I haven't dealt with I usually write about the situation and the feelings tied to it. The fear, doubt, pain, whatever it is. Then I pray about whether God intends for me to speak with the person or confront it in another way or simply let it go. Sometimes I write a letter and mail or hand-deliver it, other times I tear it up or burn it. Either way, it's out of my house which helps me to move out of the valley. The process helps me release unforgiveness and stand firm if the emotion or person tries to re-enter when they are not intended to be in my life. It also helps me to identify when I am dealing with a person that I am intended to love and pray for from a distance, at least for a season. After cleaning my spiritual house, I can mentally hang a notice on my spiritual door to remind myself and negative emotions that "you don't live here anymore." I went through these steps to get rid of any bitter roots. I found some roots of shame, feeling that maybe I could or should have done something differently over the years that would have put us on a different path. I found roots of doubt and fear. I believed that God was able, and He could turn this around, but there was a small part of me that doubted that He would and feared that He wouldn't. Those two emotions were planted like a tree whose roots had unexpectedly made their way into the foundation creating cracks that made way for pity. They were causing some of the feelings of sadness and of being crushed in my very house. At times, it was as if my house was empty, hollow and I was alone. At other times it was like the walls were falling in on me.

The truth of God's words helped me remove the clutter. *"I will not leave you or forsake you. Be strong and courageous, for you shall cause this people to inherit the land that I swore to their fathers to give them. Only be strong and very courageous, being careful to do according to all the law that Moses my servant commanded you. Do not turn from it to the right hand or to the left, that you may have good success wherever you go. This Book of the Law shall not depart from your mouth, but you shall meditate on it day and night, so that you may be careful to do according to all that is written in it. For then you will make your way prosperous, and then you will have good success. Have I not commanded you? Be strong*

get up and go!

and courageous. *Do not be frightened, and do not be dismayed, for the Lord your God is with you wherever you go."*

Focusing on the truth of these words helped me to get to the source of the bitter roots and pull them out one by one. God didn't put any of these emotions in my house. In fact, He sent His son to pay the price for all of them. His truth helped me turn from shame to surrender, from having closets filled with doubt to focusing on our destiny, from having a pity party to being filled with praise, and from being crushed to feeling courageous.

Once all the bitter roots had been pulled out, I could imagine the gaping holes they left. Huge gaps in the foundation, closets, and walls of my spiritual house that if left unattended to could allow other things to come in. Then I could envision God's truth filling every one of the gaps leaving me with a solid spiritual house.

It was time for me to "get up and go." God showed me that all the other experiences had to happen. Each one played a part in equipping me for this storm. No mistake I had made would be wasted. Each was used build a new spiritual muscle that made me, and our family stronger, wiser. And when all else failed, when everything I thought I controlled or knew seemed lost or irrelevant, when I felt weak, He was my strength. He was my rock, and my salvation and His grace was more than enough.

I walked back into the hospital and feeling strong and courageous. New ideas were running through my head. If the plan was for Te'ashia to be here longer, then we would make the most of it. I spoke with the doctors and nurses and reminded them that the last doctor on her rotation had put in a request for her to be moved to a larger room once one became available. I pressed until she was moved and told her that we would make this like her first apartment. And unlike a real apartment, she would have room service and could order her meals. We brought up plants and continued to use essential oils in the room. Lavender, peppermint, orange or a combination filled the space. Inspirational quotes filled the walls. Photos of our family were put up. The natural light coming through the room helped so much. We removed the bland tan hospital blankets and brought some soft ones with lively colors. Our aunt made Te'ashia a beautiful blanket in her favorite shade of purple, and she loved it the most. Nurses who had cared for her still stopped by on their breaks to say hi and see how she was doing. Little by little, she once again got her fight back.

We became the storm, not because of our strength and might, but because of our weaknesses. It was in our weakness that God's strength took over, took the lead and helped us "get up and go." Our completion in

get up and go!

this storm didn't mark the end of our journey. Instead, it indicated that these muscles were now strong and fit for the fight. Now it was time to put them to work and help others, those weak in different areas than us, as they work to build up their faith muscles.

I learned that when we choose to "get up and go" we take hold of the storm, instead of it taking hold of us. Once we take hold of it, we become it.

We become the storm by choosing to allow our adversities to make us better instead of bitter.
Bitterness doesn't just show up. Like many other emotions, it's sneaky and creeps in slowly. Once inside of you, its root digs deep into your foundation and feeds on your joy. Often bitterness comes from being or feeling mistreated or victimized by another person. It can also come from grief, pain, and sadness. If they are not confronted, bitter roots make way for other emotions that eat away at us. These roots are often covered with sharp, prickly spines like those on a cactus. Those spines can cause puncture wounds and pain to those around us whenever they try to get close. It's only by placing these roots in God's hands that they can be pulled out for good. Learning to talk to Him and put our trust in Him allows God to change us, and not just our circumstances. That's when we begin to become better, instead of bitter.

We become the storm by focusing on our purpose instead of our pain. Before Jesus was crucified on the cross, He told His disciples and followers that they were about to go through a time of great pain and sorrow. He compared it to a woman during childbirth. Jesus used this as an example in John 16: 20-21 to teach us that like a woman in those moments, we will experience pain and anguish, but it will turn to joy after her child is born. The pain from life's storms are the contractions that make way for something new to be born. Our pain will often open doors to help others who are going through a similar situation. Remembering these things will help us focus on the purpose, instead of the pain.

We become the storm by not allowing doubt to stand in the way of our destiny. Our doubt is confronted and eliminated by growing our faith. If you are in a storm, you are in the exact location where faith is built. The first step is to stop looking at faith as something you just don't have. Instead, consider it as a seed planted inside of you, a seed that God is using your circumstances to water. Faith comes by hearing the word of God and applying it to your life. If you want your faith to be stronger, and you want to trust God when it's hard, to stand strong in any storm, there are no

get up and go!

shortcuts. Be intentional about getting close to God in the places where faith is built. Get in His word, spend time, simply talking and praying to Him. Listen to music and motivational messages that inspire and keep your heart and mind on God. That is how your faith is watered, that's how it will grow. That is when you will walk away from doubt and step into your destiny.

We become the storm by using our circumstances to transform us from being crushed to courageous. Wine is made when grapes go through a crushing process. The same is true with olive oil that is made from crushing olives. Once the crushing is complete, the grapes are separated from the resulting juice, and the olives are separated from the oil they produce to complete the transformation process. We too go through the crushing process; however, to be fully transformed, we must also go through a separation process. We must allow the negative fragments that were stirred up during the crushing to be separated from our being. We must allow God to separate us from the past, separate us from our fears, remove unforgiveness and other negative thoughts and emotions so we can walk in the fullness of the courage produced by our crushing.

We become the storm when we shift our focus from pity to praise. I refuse to have a pity party! I may not like the situation, I may not understand God's plan, but I trust Him. I may be crying when I do, I may be angry or sad in the middle of it, but I'm gonna praise Him anyway!

Warrior, you are the storm!

get up and go!

Chapter 8

New Beginning

God uses the storms of life to transform us from who we have become, to who we were created to be.
Tyila Cooks

Unlike the relatively brief winds, hail, and other effects endured during severe weather that we faced with our son, this storm would rage on. Sometimes our new beginning is the start of a different chapter in our life's story. Other times it's the gift of waking up on a new day, equipped with the wisdom of new tools for the journey.

Everyone faces storms in their lives. I hope that this book has equipped you with a few tools for your survival kit. After all, each of us is either in a storm, coming out of a storm or heading for a storm of various intensity and severity. The goal is to be prepared when inclement weather hits. And remember, you are not alone! Others have walked this path before, some walk as you walk and still others will come behind you. Each will at times experience loneliness, sadness, fear, anger, pain, grief, and fatigue while yearning for peace, joy, hope, and love. Still, I'm confident that each person who learns to stay close to God, to put their trust in Him no matter the emotion they feel, will have the ability to "get up and go." And with that, from one eagle to another, here are some additional tools for you to add to your survival kit as we confront the truth about the common emotions faced in a storm.

Loneliness

Loneliness is a dark and complex emotion that often comes from feeling isolated. There have been times on my journey that I have felt this emotion, and I know my daughter has. Times that I didn't feel connected with others around me and I felt like God had left me. During those moments I asked myself where He was and why I couldn't see or hear Him. Why was it that His light didn't seem to be shining on me? I now compare those times to one of the worst storms that I ever drove in. The sky was dark, the rain came down like a sheet, and there was thick fog that made it impossible to see the cars around me. I was even more anxious at the thought that if I couldn't see the other drivers, they surely could not see me. In those moments, I couldn't see the side of streets well enough to pull over. The sound of the rain and hail hitting my car was so loud that I couldn't hear anything but the storm. That's just how some of my life storms have been. Dark with emotions pouring down like sheets of rain. My mind cluttered with thoughts that filled it like a fog. So much noise that I couldn't hear God. I felt alone. I now know that it's because of these times, times that we cannot see, and we cannot hear that God teaches us to walk by faith and not by sight. 2 Corinthians 5:7, "For we walk by faith, not by sight." It's not always easy to walk by faith during such difficulty. It takes courage and a desire to let go of every ounce of control that we

get up and go!

seemingly have. It will also take you on a journey that will allow you to experience God and the fullness of His grace.

Walking by faith means that you will allow God to use your tears to water the dreams He has planted in your heart, even when you feel like they have been uprooted and thrown away. It will help you find your focus, even when you feel like you have been robbed of something that was precious to you and your world has been turned upside down. Walking by faith will help you find strong determination to follow God's plan regardless of what debris your storm throws your way. It will give you the courage to stand up for the hurting, broken, and down-trodden. Walking by faith will release God from the cramped little box that you have put Him in so that His power can go to work in your life. Just like when we were learning to walk, with each new life lesson there is a lot of falling, there will be missteps, and at times, we will get ahead of ourselves. That's all part of the process. Over time, our steps will become steadier. Our balance will become stronger, and confidence will build. The first step is to be willing to move our feet. Even when we are crippled with other emotions and the winds from the storm are blowing against us, we must have a willingness to keep moving forward. Psalms 23 tells us that we were intended to walk through the valley of the shadow of the dead, not get stuck there. Allowing ourselves to stay in a dark place opens the door of our heart and mind to pity and a host of other emotions. As hard as it can be, you must choose to take the first step. Even if it is unsteady, and if you stumble, get right back up and try again.

Open your bible. This emotion, like every negative emotion, does not come from God. To find His truth go straight to His word. If the whole bible is too overwhelming for you to search through, find a book of God's promises to stand on. These can be found in bookstores and online. They pull out scriptures and organize them in a way that is easy to digest. Often you will find the exact emotion you are experiencing in the table of contents leading to several scriptures revealing the truth.

Visualize God's presence. Too often we go through the day as if God did not even exist. We are full of self-sufficiency; we make our plans and schedules and live out our days without any conscious need for His presence. Occasionally we pray, read a devotion or even listen to inspirational music. But are we walking in God's presence? It's usually in the darkness that we seek to be in His presence as if His presence is somewhere outside of our realm. Visualizing God's presence is making a deliberate choice to focus on Him. It's waking up and saying, "Good morning, God" and staying focused on Him throughout the day. It's

get up and go!

envisioning Him walking beside us, making each decision with us, holding our hand, wiping our tears and embracing us when we need it most. It means we communicate within the darkness and the light and we respond to Him always.

Expect God to keep His promises. God promises that all our needs will be met in Christ through His riches in Glory. Not just some needs will be met, but all of them. Expecting God to do what He has promised means that we realize we cannot get through this with our power and strength, but with the power of the Holy Spirit all things are possible. When we rest in this truth and believe God is faithful, we begin to experience God's presence.

Sadness

Sadness or distress, whether caused by loss, affliction, trouble, disappointment, regret or anything else, can be difficult to manage. At times it seems to just sneak up on you, take hold and cling to your spirit like a staticky skirt clings to pantyhose. No matter what you try, you just can't seem to break free from it. Our family all had our moments battling this emotion. My husband, who takes the responsibility of covering and leading our family very seriously, was often visited by sorrow. It's a heavy burden for a man not to be able to prevent some adversities from hitting the family he guards, protects and provides for. For both of us, it was excruciating to watch one of our children endure so much pain and suffering and not to be able to take it away. For our daughter, it was a battle not to sink into a depression and give up the fight after taking such blows. We all thought that we had won the fight when we had simply won the round.

The flood of emotions such as these can put us in a pit of despair. There are times in my life that I've briefly sat in that very cold, damp, smelly pit. Each time I tried a new technique to get out and not fall in again. They were all good, helpful things, strategies to change my life's circumstances. Still, none of the external solutions I tried were lasting. That emotion always seemed to ease its way back in at some point. Then came the seed of truth that God planted in my heart. A seed that didn't take the pain of sadness away all at once, but in time, God watered it, and it began to grow strong and bear fruit. The seed was from John 16:33 where Jesus told the disciples, "In this world, you will have sorrow, but take heart I have overcome the world." Jesus didn't sugarcoat it; He didn't soften the words. He was clear and concise, in part, to prepare His disciples for what was to come.

get up and go!

With this scripture applied to my life's story, God has taught me that this life is not trouble-free. Think about it, Jesus too was a man of sorrows. He knew the pain and suffering of this life. He knew temptation, fear, illness, and death. He experienced rejection, loss, poverty, loneliness, and abuse. There is not one tear we have shed that He does not understand. So how do we break free from the sorrow, pull it out of our hearts and minds by the roots? By standing on the entire message of John 16:33. "I have told you these things, so that in me you may have peace. In this world, you will have trouble. But take heart! I have overcome the world." This scripture lets us know that Jesus took on all our sin, shame, and sorrow at the cross. He bore the weight not only of our guilt and punishment but also of our negative emotions, including sadness. When He rose from the grave, He conquered sin and death. When we put our hope and our faith in Him that's where we find our peace.

As a child of God, we can trust that He will provide for us. We can rest in the assurance that His love for us is not dependent on what we do but on what Jesus has already done. We also have the promise that God will finish what He started in us. At the end of the process, we will be forever changed for the better. He will use every pain, every sorrow, and every tear in our lives for our good and His glory. And the best part is that we don't have to go through this alone. God promises to be our strength in weakness and will give us everything we need to live for Him.

Although the visits are less frequent, sadness still tries to make an unexpected entrance occasionally. Now I identify it like I recognize that a sneeze is a sign that a cold is threatening to take hold. Just like I reach for my Airborne to head off the cold, when I notice sorrow, I reach for God's truth. I speak to this emotion and tell it, "sadness, my Father has overcome you, you have no place here."

Fear

I once saw a quote that said, "Fear is not an option, you have a choice." When I think of fear, one of the stories that come to mind is the story of Jesus' Apostle Paul in Acts 27. Paul, along with other followers of Christ and crew members were on a difficult journey to Rome. For two weeks they endured a horrific storm while they traveled by ship to their destination. In the middle of the journey, the crew was feeling helplessness and hopelessness. That's when God promised Paul through an Angel, that he would stand trial in Rome (23:11). Paul realized that he couldn't very well stand trial if he died on this journey, therefore; no matter how bad the

get up and go!

storm was, God must intend for him to live. As Paul clung to the promise, he was able to choose faith over fear which helped him to keep his eyes on God as the Captain, instead of on the frightened crew. Often when things get tough, we tend to do the opposite. We start to focus on the crew, instead of the captain. We listen to their voices or begin to look at situations and play all the possibilities in our minds repeatedly. In other words, we put more emphasis on the contributors to our story, than the author. That opens the door to fear which can cripple us. God's promises are always in His word. His truth tells us not to be frightened or dismayed and sometimes we must tell ourselves that we are not. "I am not frightened or dismayed because God is with me and He holds me and helps me." God is asking us, especially in our storms, to depend on Him completely. Can that be scary? Of course, it can. Do it anyway!

When God asks something of us, we have a choice. Are we going to allow fear to slip inside our spiritual house through a window or are we going to stand on faith? God's plan will ultimately succeed either way. The question is, will you be at peace during the process or will you come out of the storm and look back to see that it wasn't the storm that caused destruction, it was fear? Another truth is that most of the things we fear never happen anyway. This acronym puts fear in its proper place.

False
Evidence
Appearing
Real

Always remember that you have a choice!

Anger

Most everyone must deal with anger at one point or another. It's characteristics often include hostility, displeasure, wrath and sometimes vengeance. There is a dramatic difference between acknowledging and responding to our anger and reacting to it. There have been so many times in my journey that I have been faced with this emotion. Like the other bitterness that I mentioned, Anger is the fruit of rotten roots. At times they were the roots of strife, impatience or seemingly unmet needs. In the storms with our children I faced all of these, but most often it has been an injustice that threatened to take root. I wanted the situations to change because they didn't seem fair. For God to use these circumstances for His glory, I had to face anger and deal with it. I had to admit that I don't always

get up and go!

understand why things must happen, I don't like watching my children suffer, yet I cannot change it. That's where the digging begins. Whatever your truth is, wherever your pain stems from, admitting it instead of masking it will help you start exposing it. Digging deep to get to the bad root is painful, but it's the only way to take care of the problem for good.

You may have a good reason for being angry, but don't use it as an excuse to stay that way. Instead of denying or justifying it, ask God to help you admit it and deal with it positively. The emotion of anger is never given to us by God and pulling out the exposed root can be a battle.

Ephesians 6:12 tells us that we wrestle not against flesh and blood, but against principalities, against powers, against the rulers of the darkness of this world, against spiritual wickedness in high places. To me, this means that Satan is our real enemy. He uses storms in our lives as an opportunity to plant negative emotions in us to keep us from accomplishing the will of God in our lives. When we become angry or if we have unresolved anger, talking to God and admitting it is the first step. He already knows anyway, and this helps you to get to the root, pray over the source, pull it out and fill that space with healing, forgiveness or whatever your truth is. Take the first step, and God will take care of the rest.

Pain

When it comes to pain, we are just as vulnerable to emotional and spiritual blows as we are when our bodies are impacted by physical blows. Often, we learn from the world that physical pain is acceptable, but that emotional pain is not. Walking around on crutches or with your arm in a sling is accepted but talking about your feelings for too long isn't. As a result, we sometimes try to reject or hide our emotional pain.

The truth is that even Jesus experienced emotional pain. When He, our greatest example, heard that Lazarus had died. Jesus saw the anguish of His family and friends as He too experienced some of these same emotions. When this happened, Jesus didn't hold it in; He didn't try to hide the way He was feeling. Instead, John 11 tells us that "He wept," which lets us know that Jesus cares deeply about our hurts and He knows that we will encounter experiences that are very painful. Remember that in John 16:33 Jesus was clear that in this world we would have trouble. His examples show us that we aren't expected to hide our feelings. God knows that sometimes the pain will be so great that we too will cry. When we do Psalms 56:8 tells us that God keeps track of our sorrows, collects our tears in a bottle, records each in His book.

get up and go!

During Ancient Roman times tear catchers were commonly used by mourners. They would fill beautiful, lavishly decorated glass bottles with their tears and lovingly placed them in tombs as a symbol of respect, remorse, love and grief for the deceased. It was believed that the greater the amount of tears collected in bottles indicated how important the deceased was. Imagine that these mourners worked to catch many tears to show their respect and our Father has so much adoration and love for us that He catches EVERY tear and records it in His book. I believe He uses those very tears to water our hopes and dreams.

Yes, in this world you will experience pain, but with God, you will never experience it alone, and none of it will be wasted. Hidden pain does not do anyone any good, but pain in God's hands can be used for something amazing. You can't change what happened to you, but you can allow God to use it for your good and His purposes.

Our family still prays for the donor family and tears fill my eyes when I think about the precious gifts our daughter has received. Mostly I pray that they know the magnitude of God's love and understand the purpose that comes from the pain. Even as we continue to battle, I have a better understanding of the purpose. When I think about our journey, I know that those who have been the most sympathetic are those who traveled down a similar road as us. A person who has endured and survived the heartbreak of divorce can best help someone experiencing it now. Someone who had faced financial hardships or bankruptcy can best provide wisdom and a listening ear to a person encountering it. Those who have overcome the pain of abuse or molestation can best guide others out of a similar valley.

Your greatest ministry, your ability to help others will come from strength gained through your pain and weaknesses.

Grief

Grief is such a tough emotion. It is a natural response to the loss of a someone or something like your health, a marriage, a job, a beloved pet or anything that's important to you. As we grieve, we may feel any variety of emotions, and there is no one size fits all approach. No matter how much money we have or how good a life we live, there is no way to avoid facing grief at one time or another. The goal, as I see it, is to simply lean on God and to keep moving your feet one tiny step at a time, so you don't get stuck in a dark place. Grieving is an individual process, everyone does it

get up and go!

differently and for different lengths of time. One of the first steps to conquering it acknowledging and understanding it.

Most believe that grief comes in stages and I have found this to be true. There are various opinions on how many steps there are; however, most agree that the following are included in some capacity. I have added a few examples to help paint the picture of how a person who is grieving may be feeling.

1. Denial: Often, denial results in feelings of plain shock or disbelief when you first learn of a loss. It's our body's natural way of resisting or rejecting the situation to protect ourselves.

2. Anger: When the gravity and reality of the situation begin to set in, pain is usually the next emotion we feel, and at times it's quickly followed by anger. Part of the process is to face the pain and frustration that we are experiencing.

3. Bargaining: This is often the place where feelings of regret slip in. Many times, at this stage people ask themselves what they could have done to change or prevent the situation.

4. Depression: This is where sadness sets in as you begin to understand the loss and its effect on your life. Feelings of regret and loneliness are usually a part of this place in the journey. Also, people in this stage often find themselves with a decreased appetite; they have difficulty sleeping and bouts of crying are common. Some may feel overwhelmed and lonely.

5. Acceptance: This is the final stage of grief. It's a place where people begin to accept their reality. It doesn't mean that we don't still feel sad. It simply means that we're able to start moving forward with our lives. We're able to begin reinvesting the time that we used to spend on the person or situation we have been grieving over. Now, instead of using it to grieve, it is spent on something else or someone else. We spend it on ourselves and the future.

Every person will experience these stages in his or her own way. They may go back and forth between them before they reach acceptance or skip some stages altogether. At times, a memory, song or important anniversary can start the cycle over again.

One of my greatest moments of grief was when I received that call from my uncle back in 2011 telling me that my father was not only dead but that he had taken his own life. I was devastated. First by the thoughts of my father's loss, then the gravity of the way that he died. For me, that

get up and go!

was the hardest part because for as long as I could remember, my father considered himself to be an atheist. It broke my heart to think about what this meant. I couldn't bear the thought that he had left this earth without accepting Christ into his heart.

For days I grieved and toggled between the various stages. I was angry with God and overwhelmed. Like many, I wondered how in situations like this one we could claim God was there? Where is our hope when things seem to end so badly? I blamed myself and questioned what I could have done differently. My husband watched over me and prayed for me as I went through the process. Then, after days of crying, a friend called me, and I shared my anguish, taking the first step toward facing what I was feeling.

My friend reminded me that I was not created to carry this burden. He also helped me to realize that I had done just what God asked me to do by praying for my father all these years. He went on to say that if my father couldn't see Christ in the way that my husband and I lived our lives, then he was never gonna see him through us.

After the call, I went to my prayer room, laid flat out on the floor and prayed. I asked for forgiveness for anything I could or should have done differently and for doubting God's plan. I told God that I didn't understand this, it didn't feel good or look good, but I trust Him. At that moment, the burden I had been trying to carry was lifted from me, although the grief remained. I learned that day that it was possible to grieve and still be at peace. It was that peace and God's strength that gave me the courage to get up and be there for my family. I didn't know where I was going, but I loved and trusted the One who was leading.

As days turned into weeks my grief began to dissipate, then just before Father's Day I received another call from my uncle. My uncle had been the one to go to California to help finalize things with my father's belongings. My uncle told me that next to my father's favorite chair was a stack of books, which was not surprising because he was an avid reader. He went on to say that in the stack of books was a box, and in the box was a bible. Inside that bible were scriptures that my dad had been reading and highlighting.

More than anything, this was a reassurance, a reminder to me that I don't know what happened in those days or moments of my father's life, but I know the prayers I prayed and the power of my God. It was a gift that I hadn't asked for, yet I was beyond grateful to receive it.

get up and go!

If you are experiencing grief, try not to rush the process and don't expect your feelings and emotions to be like anyone else's. By design, you are unique, and your journey will be tailored to fit you. Do remember that you weren't intended to carry this burden alone. Share your feelings with God and with others who can help. He has so much love and compassion for us, and He will help give us hope, if we let Him. Revelation 21: 4 states, "He will wipe every tear from their eyes. There will be no more death or mourning or crying or pain, for the old order of things has passed away."

Fatigue

Like me, you may become exhausted in the storm. When you are exhausted your emotions can make you feel like you're drowning. This often happens when you've been in the storm for a while, and it doesn't show signs of stopping. It's easy to be optimistic at the beginning of the inclement weather. When the rain comes, and the winds blow, often our faith is less strong. Initially, we may say things like God's got it! Weeping may endure for a night, but joy comes in the morning. But what happens when the storm rages on and on? When cancer that was in remission comes back, or the marriage that was just getting better takes another blow? When the child who has been rebelling gets into trouble again or the prognosis turns for the worse? When the bank account is empty, and the house is about to foreclose? When the storm has passed, and you're left with seemingly nothing but a pile of debris, that's when we get tired? There have been times that I have been in this place. Trying to hold my head up, trying to get up, but feeling too...tired. No matter how smart, dedicated or educated you are, you still get tired. You lay down and get up tired. You eat, drink, drive, interact with others, but you're still, tired. You walk around tired, go through your day to day routine tired, and nobody knows that you are because you put on your smile just like you put on your shoes.

We are tired, yet God has worked so hard to get us ready for that thing we've been praying for. Too often we ask for something, we pray for something, but we never really consider the cost or what it takes to get us ready for that something we prayed for. When my daughter was four years old, and I prayed that she would be free from diabetes, I never in a million years, imagined the cost or the preparation needed to receive such a blessing. I also prayed as a young girl for my husband; I never realized the cost. I didn't realize that God would take my poor choices, my mistakes, life lessons and even life's storms and press them together to prepare me to be his wife. The truth is, if I had met him first, I wouldn't have been ready. I

get up and go!

would not be the wife that he needs or deserves, and I wouldn't appreciate him the way I do. If we're not careful, if we miss this, we won't keep our eyes on God. The storm we were meant to go through, will get inside of us and make us tired. Our tired emotions will trick us and will lead us down the wrong road. They will get inside of our mind, our heart, and our will and pull us down like magnet adhering to metal.

There is nothing wrong with being tired. Most of us have been so strong that we survived in water that we should have drowned in a long time ago. And now, when we should be celebrating that we're moving in on that finish line, we're exhausted. Often when a person is exhausted, and they feel like they're drowning. If we're not careful our exhaustion will make us lash out at people who are trying to help us, make us doubt people we can trust and make us feel scared when we're safe. They will make us hold on to what's familiar instead of holding on to God's promises. I believe that our greatest example, Jesus felt every one of the emotions mentioned in this chapter. When He did, I believed He allowed the Holy Spirit to take the lead.

Jesus made sure His own emotions, passions, and desires yielded to what the Holy Spirit wanted. Yielding also helped Him focus on God's promises instead life's problems. With this choice, Jesus opened the door to truth, and it allowed love to replace loneliness, joy to replace sadness, peace to replace anger, and faith to replace fear. He also allowed pleasure to replace pain, happiness to replace grief, and livelihood to replace fatigue. All of this made people want a relationship with Him, and He was positioned for God to work through Him to help those around Him. I believe this was His greatest praise to God. It can be ours too.

God has given you the gifts of gratitude and peace, have you opened them?

Once we were home from our summer stay at the hospital, I sat down to sort through stacks of mail and paperwork that I had gotten behind on. I was reminded that much of this book was written as we went through our storms. As I sorted, I came across notes that I had jotted down on the back of envelopes, slips of paper, parking tickets and such. These were pieces of the puzzle that captured critical moments like the scribbled message and instructions from that wonderful call we received back in June. There were the notes telling of Te'ashia's progress at various times throughout this journey. Next, were slips of paper about TMA and AHUS, creatinine levels, platelet counts, glucose levels, white blood cell and hemoglobin levels. There were tear stained prayers and scriptures, and a

get up and go!

decal that hung on her wall at the hospital. They helped me recall the many nurses who came into her room sharing their personal stories or offering and seeking encouragement. I thought about the chaplain sent by one of the doctors to comfort me when we first learned about the AHUS diagnosis. After we talked for a while, the chaplain mentioned how encouraging our conversation had been *for them* and asked if it was possible to return later in the week. Then I came across a discharge summary and new orders for more dialysis because of the struggling kidney. I found a laundry list of prescriptions and many, many more appointments and infusions that would be required for the next year. There was an emergency dialysis packet should we need to move to another center after the impending hurricane hit. Next, I found a note that I jotted down after speaking with one of her doctors who said that the AHUS seemed to be controlled. I located an old appointment reminder card for the procedure that Te'ashia had to have done in early October when her Hemodialysis Catheter came out as she slept. I remember her describing how shocked the nurses were when she walked into the clinic holding it in her hand. They rushed her to a seat, called the doctor and had the ambulance on standby. According to them, when this happens most people bleed to death in their sleep, yet Te'ashia didn't lose a single drop of blood. Then I found a parking ticket from the day we went to the transplant clinic in late October. That's when a member of the transplant team told us that her new kidney wasn't going to regain its function, she would have to be re-listed for another transplant. That was also the day I asked God to blow their minds and show Himself strong, knowing with everything in my being that He alone was in control.

The following week, after being readmitted for an infection, the original transplant doctor who treated her after the surgery stepped into her room looking a bit emotional. He was there to tell us that the blood work they had run for the last two days showed that her kidney was starting to function, and he wanted to suspend her dialysis to see if it could sustain on its own. I wanted to shout right there! All I could think of was Shirley Caesar's song, I Feel Like Praising Him! Anyone who has heard this song knows what I mean when I say, "I needed somebody to hold my mule!"

The doctor went on to say, "I have been there since the beginning of this, and I have been one of the doctors who has followed your case all along. I cannot tell you how happy I am for you, your mother and your

get up and go!

family, I know what you have been through." As I came to the end of my stack of papers, I realized that I was soaked with my own tears.

That stack of papers was like opening the gifts of gratitude and praise all over again. I was overwhelmed with praise for God just wanting to have a relationship with me. He chose me, and I choose Him, over and over again. I love Him with my whole heart, and I am beyond grateful that He trusts unworthy me and has found me to be a useful instrument to fulfill His purposes.

That was the first week of November 2017. Since then Te'ashia has completely come off dialysis, and we are living in a bit of a calm, comparatively speaking. So calm that I often wake up in tears, filled with praise and gratitude that I slept through the night without giving thought to Te'ashia having low blood sugar or what condition I might find her in the next morning. And while our schedule is still very hectic, we are enjoying fewer trips to Atlanta and three fewer appointments for dialysis. Now, we have a much greater appreciation for living in the moment, knowing that the next one is not promised to any of us. We also have a renewed excitement about our next home, our heavenly home, and we have loosened our grasp some on this one. And now, I see Te'ashia as my daughter again, and not a patient. I hadn't even realized that I had begun to see her through different lenses until a friend pointed out something similar about a loved one she was caring for. As a caregiver, especially a long-term caregiver, we can tend to focus on day to day appointments and tasks rather than seeing our loved one through God's eyes. When this happens something very special can get lost in the mix. As a result, circumstances can overshadow all of the endearing qualities that you enjoy about your loved one. It's also important for caregivers to pre-empt burnout by asking for help when it's needed. We permit ourselves to take breaks, take care of and take time for ourselves (even if we must wake up a little earlier to do it). And for both the patient and the caregiver, it's important to listen more than we speak, find reasons to laugh out loud often and to lead with love.

Just when we thought we might ease into the next year, God had one final gift for us. Now that the life-threatening needs are stable, we have been able to focus on Te'ashia's vision loss. When she lost vision in her right eye back in 2015, she was to have surgery and injections to repair the Macular Edema and detached retina completely. Over the course of

get up and go!

the last year, she gradually lost all vision in her left eye, and some loss has reoccurred in the right eye.

We had hoped that visits to two specialists would leave us with promising news about the possibility of a similar repair. Instead, we learned of yet another approaching storm, Ischemic Optical Neuropathy (damage to the optic nerve of the eye). The doctor ran several tests, and as we waited, I texted my newest sister friend after they shared the possible prognosis with us. She is a daughter of the King who God has unexpectedly placed in my path. My friend has lovingly labored with us in prayer over the months and promised to do the same with this. Even though she sent me a word of encouragement, for a few moments I just felt numb. Not angry, not sad, just numb. Then I began to feel sad for my daughter. I knew I needed some time away from her to process this and get my head ready for whatever fight we were about to face, but at that moment I didn't have the luxury.

As I sat next to my daughter, trying so hard to stay focused and not let her see my emotions, I started to leak. She looked over to ask me a question and said, "are you crying?" "About this?" I couldn't even answer her. I just sat quietly. That's when she said, "mom, they said I had neuropathy in my legs, and it improved. They said, my kidney wouldn't work, and it does." Then she gave me the biggest smile and said, "and even if God decides to take my vision away, I have a brand-new pancreas, so I don't mind learning to fold my dollars like Ray Charles! And I think I deserve an eggnog milkshake as a treat after all this". We laughed so hard. I wanted to holler! Right there in the waiting room. This girl, I just love her. I love how she has grown, and I love her humor. Most of all I love how God has changed her and helped her to rely on Him, to trust in Him for herself. After running the tests, the doctor confirmed that her condition is ION. He was very empathetic, and he looked at Te'ashia and said, "I hope 2018 is better for you, Lord knows you had a hard enough time this year". Without missing a beat, she said, "oh, I had a great year, and 2018 is gonna be even better!"

So here we are at the end this chapter, yet surely others will be written. As I conclude this book and prepare to write another, I am in awe of my God, my Father. Just like when I read Psalms 139, I cannot read these pages without being overwhelmed by the glimpses of God's glory, majesty, miracles, and wonders that I have had the privilege of seeing up close and personal.

As I prepare to send my draft to the editor I am thinking of all that I didn't capture in these pages, yet if just one finds hope when they feel like

get up and go!

there is none, it will have served its purpose. My new beginning comes with the knowledge that I am forever changed. Still, I know that this butterfly will go back into the cocoon again and again, for the rest of my days. The process may not feel good, but baby, there is nothing like earning your wings. There is nothing like realizing that the greatest gifts don't come from God changing our circumstances, they come from God changing us. It is this change that brings us closer to Him, the center of our joy.

get up and go!